BROUGHT TO YOU BY:

_____

_____

"YOU CAN'T MOTIVATE OTHER PEOPLE."

Nothing could be further from the truth. In fact, the highest paid professionals on the planet get paid to motivate other people. It is a high ART, starting with motivating ourselves.

If I were to ask you what you would LOVE to do tomorrow if you had three magic wishes, just in answering the question … tapping into your imagination … your conversation with yourself would change, your body chemistry would change, your hormone balance would change, your physical appearance, posture, and strength would change, and most importantly, what you would be *willing* to do would change in an instant.

All of those changes in your body and mind make up Motivation. Motivation is *energy*. And we can create it in other people just by the questions we ask them. In fact, as leaders, it is job number two. Creating it in ourselves is job number one.

"SELF-MOTIVATION. WITHOUT IT, NOTHING ELSE WORKS. WITH IT, NOTHING ELSE MATTERS."

— **Richard Bliss Brooke**

ENDORSEMENTS

"I just read your *Mach2* book, and it is a masterpiece … head and shoulders above the rest of the motivation books I have read."

— Harvey Mackay

Author of the bestselling books *Swim with the Sharks Without Being Eaten Alive* and *The Mackay MBA of Selling in the Real World*

"I love *Mach2 With Your Hair On Fire*. I could tell when I read the book that Richard has a passion for changing people's lives. I respect Richard and his work and thank him for who he is and the difference and impact he's making in people's lives and businesses."

— Les Brown

Author of the bestselling book *Live Your Dreams*

"If you are committed to extraordinary success, *Mach2* is a must-have for your personal library! The information on Vision and Self-Motivation is some of the best you will find anywhere."

— Bob Proctor

Author of the bestselling book *You Were Born Rich*

"*Mach2* is terrific! Not only is it a 'must read' for the brand new Network Marketing distributor, it is destined to be the handbook for seasoned veterans of the industry."

— Tom Chenault

Host of *The Home-Based Business* radio show and daily prime time radio show *Business for Breakfast*

"Many students of success write about it, second-hand. Richard Brooke, a master mentor, writes about success as he has experienced it. There is a life-altering gem of wisdom on every page. Read, internalize and positive change will materialize."

— Denis Waitley

Author, *The Psychology of Winning*

"Richard Brooke's *Mach2* is a fast-moving, entertaining book full of fast, funny, helpful ideas on success and achievement."

— Brian Tracy

Author, *Goals!*

"In this accelerated economy you have to travel at *Mach2*. This book teaches you how to do it in an omni-effective and fun way."

— **Mark Victor Hansen**

Co-creator, #1 *New York Times* bestselling series *Chicken Soup for the Soul* and Co-author, *The One Minute Millionaire*

"I've read and reviewed most every book on personal development there is. I only give credence to books written by authors whose lives are a testimony to the principles they preach. I want to know the success principles that elevated someone from a chicken cutter earning $3.05 an hour to a multi-millionaire … and you will too! In *Mach2*, Richard shares timeless principles to help you find the courage, motivation and pathway to greater success."

— **Darren Hardy**

Publisher, *SUCCESS* magazine

"The example of Richard Brooke's dynamic, visionary leadership is what first awakened my interest in the field of Network Marketing. As his book makes clear, he's committed to inspiring people – even outside his great company."

— **Scott DeGarmo**

Author of *Heart to Heart* & former Editor-in-Chief, *SUCCESS* magazine

"I found a copy of *Mach2* at a friend's house. I read and loved it. So much of what the great athletes do to accomplish the impossible is done through visualization. Richard captures exactly how it works, why it works, and how anyone can use it to do great things in their life. Richard has a unique way of telling the story so we all really get it!"

— **John Elway**

Super Bowl MVP & NFL Hall of Fame Quarterback
President of Football Operations/General Manager – Denver Broncos

"I can sincerely say that Richard Brooke has changed my way of thinking more than anyone. I will always be grateful to Richard for making me a better person."

— **Gale Sayers**

NFL Hall of Fame Running Back – Chicago Bears

"Before every game, I would visualize how I would react in different situations on the ice. *Mach2* will teach you how visualization can separate you from the rest and give you the edge needed to succeed."

— **Adam Deadmarsh**

2002 Olympic Silver Medalist, Hockey; Stanley Cup Winner, Colorado Avalanche; Stanley Cup Playoff MVP, Los Angeles Kings

"Richard Brooke's *Mach2* is extraordinary. I loved it."

— **Dan Quayle**
44th Vice President of the United States

"I loved *Mach2*. Richard captures the laws of attraction and action wonderfully. I am giving it to all my agents."

— **John Beutler**
#1 Agent in the world for Century 21, 2003 & 2005

"I recommend *Mach2* to everyone. The book offers many points to ponder. One of my favorites is the distinction of knowing who you are and where you want to go in your life. You must DECIDE and ACT."

— **Bill Morrow**
Owner of 17 Red Robin restaurants
Founder, The Quarry at La Quinta & Branson Creek Golf Club

"Absolutely incredible!"

— **John Addison**
Former Co-CEO of Primerica, the largest term life insurance
company in the world; Author of *Real Leadership*

"Passion and a belief in each individual's potential seem to jump out of Richard Brooke's book. Reading it is both adventurous and a career map."

— **Rick Goings**
Former Chairman & CEO, Tupperware Brands Corporation;
Former President, Avon Germany and Avon USA

"I work with the Franklin-Covey organization in their Personal Coaching Division. We handled the coaching for the Napoleon Hill Foundation, Tom Hopkins, Denis Waitley, Zig Ziglar, Brian Tracy and Stephen Covey. Richard's book quickly became a 'must read' item for our team. It has been a powerful tool in my personal life and I have watched it plant that all-important seed of hope and belief into other people's lives."

— **Dennis Walker**
Salt Lake City, UT

"I got a lot from *Mach2* and borrowed some of Richard's quotes for an offsite strategy session I facilitated. This book is so good that I ordered a few copies for my friends and family."

— **Charles Orr**
Former President, Shaklee Corporation
Direct Selling Association Hall of Fame member

"*Mach2* is absolutely brilliant. I don't know a person in the world who wouldn't benefit from reading it and building a bigger vision, then manifesting it into their life!"

— **Randy Gage**

Author of *Risky is the New Safe* and *Mad Genius*

"Vision is the cornerstone of all achievement. And Richard Brooke's *Mach2* is far and away the most clear, compelling, complete and immediately useful, results-getting work on vision ever written!"

— **John Milton Fogg**

Founder of *Upline*® & *Network Marketing Lifestyles*;
Author of *The Greatest Networker in the World,* and *The Inner Game of Network Marketing*

"Richard Brooke captures the essence of success principle No. 1: You've got to believe it before you will see it. Through his own experiences, he comes to life in a brilliantly simple, thought-provoking, powerful message about developing a new belief system. He grabs you from page one."

— **Carol Anton**

The number ONE Sales Director in the world, Retired Mary Kay, Inc.

"Richard Brooke is the consummate mentor and storyteller, and *Mach2* can be the roadmap for changing your whole life! I enthusiastically recommend this compelling personal story that is sure to touch your heart and mind."

— **Dave Johnson**

31-year Network Marketing Veteran & Nikken Royal Ambassador

"Richard Brooke's *Mach2* has helped members of our global leadership team forge compelling visions, master their own motivation, and create tangible results at Mach2 speed!"

— **Art Jonak**

Founder of the Mastermind Event

"Richard Brooke is one of my favorite Masters of Network Marketing. Little did I know when I first received the *Mach2* manuscript in 1997 what a huge impact it would have on my life, both in business and personal. All these years later, his words are still invaluable to me!"

— **Jackie Ulmer**

Lake Arrowhead, CA

"I've been a student of Richard Brooke since 1995, when I was introduced to his work through a Vision Workshop. Hearing *Mach2* on audio is like reliving that workshop and getting the power of repetition and reinforcement. The first CD alone I listened to three times to get the strategies for creating a vision locked in, so I could pass them on to people I meet around the world. I will recommend *Mach2* as long as I have breath."

— Mark "Google Superman" Davis
Public Speaker, Coach & Author of *The Internet Success Secret*

"Richard Brooke is an articulate and powerful motivator. *Mach2* has substance, relevance and will make a positive difference in the lives of those wise enough to use its principles. Plus, it's a fun read."

— Rudy Revak
President & Founder, Symmetry Corporation

"Our work at Human Potential is intended to help companies shape their future. This involves work on values, vision, mission, strategy and generating the competence to implement them. Our clients include companies like Microsoft, Intel, EDS, Capital One and Amgen. *Mach2* is a must-read for anyone who wants to get it quickly, clearly and powerfully!"

— Chris Majer
CEO, Human Potential Project

"Richard Brooke is that rarest phenomenon: a philosopher who spends as much time working as thinking. The result is a book that has been lived and is a life success guide that keeps it real. Real world, real time, real practical and powerful."

— Clifton H. Jolley, PhD
President, Advent Communications

"I have a copy of *Mach2* that I read once in a while when I need a funny, focused dose of the Law of Attraction. The LOA is everywhere, but this is one of the first works that speaks about it in other-than-secret terms."

— Richard Lanoue
Amazon Book Review Beaumont

"Richard Brooke has polished the art of motivating people who are unsatisfied with their lives. He condenses a life of work and teaching into a manual for CHANGE through embracing vision and motivation … the most solid formula for achieving success in finding and becoming the person you want to be."

— Grady Harp
Rated as a Top 10 Reviewer, Amazon.com

"*Mach2* is a must-read for anyone in a Network Marketing business. It offers a very clear explanation of the Law of Attraction without the cloak and dagger of other popular books. I especially love his definition of vision. Read the book. It's worth every penny!"

— A. Cummings

"I have become an evangelist for *Mach2*! It is a very informational read. I share this book with my business prospects so they will have a tool to transform their lives and reach whatever goals they choose."

— Mark Beaumier, Jr.
Painesville, OH

"Richard Brooke is well-known in my organization for many years. I bought hundreds of copies of *Mach2* in Russian translation, and this outstanding book has rendered enormous influence on the outlook of my downline."

— Roman Sobolevsky
Lvov, Ukraine

"Richard Brooke's *Mach2* is the most valuable gift I have ever received. His personal story and interesting analogies truly reach his readers!"

— Young Song
Korea

MACH2

WITH YOUR HAIR ON FIRE

HOW TO MASTER SELF-MOTIVATION & STAY ON FIRE FOR LIFE

RICHARD BLISS BROOKE

ISBN # 0-970039-1-3
Published by Bliss Business, LLC
1875 North Lakewood Drive, Suite 300
Coeur d'Alene, Idaho 83814
P: 855.480.3585
Printed in the United States of America

TABLE OF CONTENTS

This is the true joy in life, being used for a purpose recognized by yourself as a mighty one. That is being a force of nature instead of a feverish, selfish little clod of ailments and grievances, complaining that the world will not devote itself to making you happy.

I am of the opinion that my life belongs to the whole community and as long as I live, it is my privilege to do for it whatever I can.

I want to be thoroughly used up when I die, for the harder I work, the more I live. I rejoice in life for its own sake. Life is no "brief candle" to me. It is a sort of splendid torch, which I have got hold of for the moment and I want to make it burn as brightly as possible before handing it on to future generations.

— George Bernard Shaw, 1856-1950
Quoted from the preface to the play *Man and Superman* (1907)

INTRODUCTION

The purpose of telling you my story is for context. What I have to say about the science of personal achievement IS personal, and my story brings these principles and strategies to life. Seeing how I may be like you, and learning what I did with these ideas, can support you in pursuing *mastery* of them.

I grew up on a large cattle ranch and farm in a little town in the San Joaquin Valley called Chowchilla. The ranch was thousands of acres and the nearest neighbor was miles away. As such, my friends were mostly animals ... horses, cows, birds, rabbits, and pollywogs. I did not grow up socializing with other kids. I did not have many birthday parties or sleepovers. It didn't help that up until the sixth grade I still wet the bed. There was one family that lived about four miles away. We used to socialize with them and I'd have the occasional sleepover. Then the oldest boy sexually assaulted me one night while I was asleep. That ended that.

My parents were mostly to be feared, as it seemed I was always doing something I was not supposed to be doing. Or maybe it was because they just yelled a lot.

Then without any notice or consulting me, we sold the ranch. Something about estate taxes. We moved to the big city of Merced, California. That was pretty much terrifying to me. My parents were staging for a divorce and I didn't have a 3,000-acre ranch on which to hide.

I got thrust into the sixth-grade social scene at Chenoweth Elementary School. Everyone there seemed so different than at my other school. They knew each other really well and hung out all the time. They were highly social. They were very cool. They had girlfriends … sort of. They had cool clothes and bikes. Although I no longer wet the bed, I did not feel like I fit in.

By that time, I was already the victim of chronic low self-esteem. I did not trust other people. I did not feel loved. I did not have confidence. I thought that in the presence of other people—especially kids my age—that what was to come was humiliation, either because I didn't know how to *be* with other kids or because I was going to wet the bed. I did not feel safe. Unless, of course, I was with the animals or the water or the clouds or the wind … there I was safe.

I survived in part because of the generosity and kindness of some of those kids. They invited me in. They accepted me. It is no coincidence that those kids, friends I met in the sixth grade, are still my very best friends. We have our own email group and we check in almost every day.

We all have a story.

Here's the deal. When we are in what's called our formative years—ages prenatal through perhaps 10 years old—we do not have enough information, experience, or context to understand everything that is happening in our worlds. We cannot make sense of it like we can now. When something happens around us now, we tap into our memories, knowledge, and rationale to have it all make sense. Even the bizarre can make some kind of sense to us when we are older. If our parents are yelling, we usually understand what it's about even if we don't know what it's about *this time*. If there is violence on TV, we tend to understand it. If someone is having a bad day, we get it.

But when we are prenatal and we hear yelling or feel fear or anxiety, we do not get it. When we are two years old and someone three times bigger than us yells NO … we do not understand *why*. We don't even understand *what* we are doing let alone why we are being yelled at.

When we are five and we want our parents' unconditional love and attention and we get rebuked, we do not associate it with them having a bad day at work. We don't know what work is.

Does that make sense?

So here is what happens. As little kids, instead of us understanding why the world around us is doing what it is doing, we decide it is about *us*. We have an experience and then we decide *who we are* because of it.

I call this "I AM-ing." *I am "this" because "this" happened.* Sometimes the experience is life-shaking, but almost always it is a simple, everyday event that as adults we wouldn't give a second thought to.

HERE ARE A FEW EXAMPLES:

Experience: At the age of 5, I stole a pair of sunglasses from Red's Market. When my mom asked me where I got them, I told her the *truth*. She made me take them back and apologize to Red.

My "I Am": *I am bad and telling the truth is a stupid thing to do.*

Experience: When I was 8, I wanted a minibike. My parents said no.

My "I Am": *I am not important … what I want is not important.*

Experience: I wet the bed almost every night until I was 10 … even as a guest in other people's homes. I was ashamed and afraid.

My "I Am": *I am an embarrassment and should not socialize overnight.*

Experience: At age 10, a girl I liked sat with me at a movie. We held hands. The very next day, she "dumped" me.

My "I Am": *I am not cool enough for the women I like … and I NEED to be cool.*

Experience: At age 10 when my parents sold the ranch—my sanctuary—it was out of my control.

My "I Am": *I am not safe, and I need to be in control.*

Experience: At all ages my parents yelled at me and "sent me to the woodshed" literally to get beaten with a board.

My "I Am": *I am not worthy of love, and I am not safe.*

ADD SOME OF YOUR OWN:

Experience: _____

_____

My "I Am":_____

_____

Experience: _____

_____

My "I Am":_____

_____

Experience: _____

_____

My "I Am": _____

_____

From these "I Am's" we form our personalities. We form our self-image. We understand how we can get hurt. We decide how we might operate to survive in life, and maybe even win. We decide who and what we are. And then we go BE in the world.

In almost every case, what we decide about ourselves is not good. It is not generous. It is not loving. It is not empowering. It is not the vision board we want to look at every day.

THE MOST COMMON I AM'S:

1. I am not good enough
2. I am not smart enough
3. I am not cool enough
4. I am not loved

5. I am not worth it (love)
6. I am bad
7. I am stupid
8. I am worthless

In every case, we make a sweeping decision about our I Am's: whether we are going to submit to them or rebel against them.

Some of us submit, meaning we live our lives as though these things are true. We play small. We are quiet. We are weak. We hide. We apologize. We seek approval constantly. We seek out others who are weak and hiding, and we join their company.

Some of us rebel, meaning we live our lives in an effort to prove these things are NOT TRUE. We rise up. We stand tall. We make sure we are seen and heard. We perform. We win. We serve. We get smart. We get wealthy. We make sure we are loved.

When it comes to motivation, those of us who *submit* tend to have mild motivation. We may want more out of life, but we won't cause a scene to get it. We tend to act out as "not deserving" and "not wanting to be seen as ambitious." We are submissive and accept our fate.

When it comes to motivation, the *rebels* get it done. They are highly motivated to achieve, and they don't mind causing a ruckus to do so. After all, they are winners.

Or are they? Here is a question worth considering: *How can it be true that I am a winner if I am always driven to prove that I am?*

The reality is that most of us are still stuck in those stories we made up decades ago. We may be responsible, intelligent, successful, and kind 50-year-olds, but too often we are still operating out of a story we made up when we were 5.

I like to think of us as bus drivers. On the bus is our family, our friends, our business colleagues, our goals and dreams, even our challenges ... the things we get to figure out how to handle in life. The bus is our life. And we have places to go, people to be, and things to do. Important things.

In all of us are two bus drivers: the miffed 5-year-old and the brilliant, all-powerful, loving and lovable 50-year-old. The Petulant Child or Superwoman.

How far we go in life, how fast we get there, how safely we get there, and how much joy we experience along the way depends on who we empower to drive the bus.

The reason I wrote *Mach2* was to teach a higher art in motivation than the reactions of a 5-year-old ... motivation not based on trying to prove something, but motivation born in spirit, in love, in passion, in creativity, in authenticity; motivation born in the knowing that we all have the power, we all have the brilliance, we all have the maturity, and we all have the *worthiness* to deserve our dreams.

There IS such a method, perhaps first articulated well by Wallace D. Wattles in *The Science of Getting Rich*, followed by Napoleon Hill in *Think and Grow Rich*, men who were before my time.

I have studied many men and women, read hundreds of books, and even invested over $250,000 in my own transformational development. In all of that I never found a book that spoke to me in the simplest of terms, in believable terms, and in a way that inspired me. Lou Tice of The Pacific Institute and Maxwell Maltz, author of *Psycho-Cybernetics*, gave me the most insight and inspiration, and my intention is to honor those works here with *Mach2*. I wrote this book for me … to help me understand what I have learned and to help me teach it to you.

CHAPTER 1
FLYING THE COOP

"EVERYONE HAS A CHICKEN PLANT IN THEIR LIFE.
AND EVERYONE CAN LEAVE IT BEHIND."

— Richard Bliss Brooke

The "I Am" decisions we make early in childhood are often irrational and random, but they can forever shape how we see ourselves and the world.

As a result of a few everyday occurrences, along with pivotal moments like my parents' divorce—these were the core beliefs I adopted early on. These beliefs became "the truth" for me ... a truth that could have lasted my whole life.

I am not good enough
I am not cool
I am not worthy of love
I am out of control
I am not safe

This didn't exactly give me a winning personality. I had a downbeat attitude, a drive to belong and to be accepted, and thanks to those sunglasses I stole at age 5, I was a compulsive liar.

I was a typical negative thinker. I hated school. I didn't study and skipped a lot of classes. I barely graduated with a D average, so I didn't even try for college.

I started my professional career pumping gas at Pearson's Arco at the corner of G and Olive Streets in Merced, California. I also lived at the gas station—in my pickup camper with Chinook, my unconditional-loving dog. The later I came home, the happier he was to see me. After I failed to lock the front door of the gas station two nights in a row, my "ambition" led me to Foster Farms, the single largest poultry processing plant in the world.

It was a union job that paid $3.05 an hour, complete with benefits, seniority, vacation, and best of all—retirement. I jumped at the opportunity. My job was to cut the chickens into parts as they flew past me on the production line ... 20,000 of them a shift. That's 38 BPM ("Birds Per Minute") for 450 to 530 minutes a day.

Even though I was a hard worker, ambitious, and intelligent, there were some aspects of my personality that held me back. I disliked most other people. I refused to let anyone I considered less competent than me ever tell me what to do. I did work my way up to teaching people how to cut up chickens, but it didn't take long for my dynamic personality to screw things up for me. I told my boss, Wayne, where he should go— and I said it in front of his boss, Mr. Hoyt. That's all it took to put me back on the production line.

Regardless, I loved the chicken plant and loved the people I worked with. At that time, I fully expected to spend the next 40 years of my life working there, building seniority (POWER), vacation time (FUN), and clicking off the years to retirement (FREEDOM). I thought I was really cutting it—life, not chickens. That was 1977. I was 22.

In May 1977, while still working in the chicken plant, I was introduced to a financial and personal development opportunity by one of my best high school buddies, Steve Spaulding, who also worked at the chicken plant.

There were several of our other high school buddies getting involved: Dave and Dan Austin, and the magnificent Jack Acker. Although we were all great guys, none of us knew anything about business, sales, wealth building, or success. We either worked in the chicken plant, the spaghetti sauce factory, sold pot, or were on unemployment. (I only worked at the chicken plant.)

And we all suffered from some form of low self-esteem. The thing about low self-esteem is that it's not always reflected in what we WANT. The five of us all wanted a Porsche. We figured at age 22 in 1977 in California, if you had a Porsche, you could get everything else you wanted!

We wanted things, but we did not believe and feel we were worthy of them. Our "wanters" worked fine but our "getters" did not. The "wanter" in us led to our joining the opportunity. But the rest was a problem.

I often marvel at how fortunate we were … fortunate to land in the hands of leaders, coaches, and mentors who specialized in transforming belief systems. Yes, they were promoting a product for profit, but more so, they were paying forward a gift once given to them. They introduced us to these age-old secrets to success and locked arms with us to lead us to learn the process. They were gifted in working with people who wanted more out of life but did not believe they could get it.

Soon after we joined, we all convened at the Ramada Inn in Bakersfield, California, for a three-day leadership event. I was so intimidated about going, I didn't have the money to go, and I was afraid of the unknown.

I went anyway.

What we all experienced that weekend was, in a word, fascinating. And in other words, it was *uplifting, inspirational, brand new, confidence-building, strategic,* and even *loving.* It launched us—all five of us—onto a new path.

None of us ever went back to the cannery or the chicken plant. Every one of our lives changed that weekend.

JIM ACKER, DAVE AUSTIN, STEVE SPAULDING, BILL LANE, RICHARD BROOKE AND JOHN CALLAHAN ON THEIR FIRST CRUISE TO THE BAHAMAS.

All of us went on to live extraordinary lives, although two were cut short. Compared to where we were and where we could have ended up, we all deployed these principles to live lives by design.

THE REST OF THE STORY

Since applying the methods in this book, my success has been significant compared to the $3.05 per hour job I started with at the chicken plant. I offer my accomplishments only for perspective. I have left so much on the table, but compared to where I started in my beliefs, I have proved that these systems work. And I've proved that … if I can do it, you can do it.

- Within six years, at age 28, I built my own sales team of 30,000 people and was earning $40,000 a month. That was 1983. In today's dollars, that is about $101,000 a month.

- I made my first million before the age of 30, advancing to the top sales leader position in a marketing organization of more than 250,000 salespeople. I was speaking to crowds of up to 3,000 and was leading 3-day transformational workshops with hundreds of participants.

- I went on to run that $50-million-per-year company at age 30 and then own my own company at age 32.

- In March 1992, at age 37, I was featured on the cover of *SUCCESS* magazine. That issue outsold every issue in their almost 100-year history.

- In 1993, I co-authored *The New Entrepreneurs: Business Visionaries for the 21st Century*.

- In 1994, I was nominated *Inc.* magazine's Entrepreneur of the Year.

- In 1995, I wrote this book. I totally rewrote it in 2018.

- In 2009, I wrote *The Four Year Career*®.

The last 20 years have been compressed with epic personal and business failures, followed by the most quantum-leap successes I have ever had the courage to imagine. And … I finally found my soul mate, Kimmy.

Together we run three global businesses from our own personal paradise in Lanai, Hawaii, including Bliss Business, a transformational coaching, workshop, and retreat organization. We are living extraordinary lives that we design.

If five guys from a small town can break out, So can you.

It's no fluke that a group of minimum wage, lower-than-low self-esteem, directionless high school buddies found their magic and power and learned how to turn it up full blast. *Mach2 With Your Hair On Fire* is about you making the same powerful discovery.

CHAPTER 2
SUCCESS DEFINED

"SUCCESS IS FALLING IN LOVE WITH THE PROCESS ...
THE DAILY TO-DOS THAT PROPEL YOU ON YOUR CHOSEN PATH."

— Richard Bliss Brooke

Do you remember when you bought your first car? Do you remember how you felt in the weeks, days, and hours leading up to the purchase … that period of time when you knew you were going to get it but were still working on financing or delivery? Do you remember the high of anticipation?

Do you remember the promise you made to yourself and others about how the car would never see rain, how you would never eat in it or abuse it in any way?

Yes, and then what happened after you got the car? Do you remember how those feelings slowly diminished?

If you were like me, it only took a couple of weeks before you were driving through mud, eating a burger and fries, and yes, back in those days, puffing away on a cigarette. Achieving the result itself had such short-lived pleasure.

Do you remember the last contest you won? Or any goal you've achieved? Think about the process leading up to it versus the actual award. The process could have lasted months, even years. But how long did the actual award last? In comparison, it is short-lived.

The essence of being truly alive comes from falling in love with the process of your dreams: always stretching, always being in momentum, and always expecting the best.

People are happiest when they're in the process of achieving, when they're accomplishing something that's tremendously important to them. It's the anticipation of getting the intended result—knowing they're on the right track and moving forward—that makes them the happiest.

Consider then, that success IS the process … the daily "doing" that leads us on our chosen path. When we choose a path, and we fall in love with the journey, every day is "new car day." Every day, we are winners. Every day, we celebrate success.

For the purpose of this book, let's say that is what we are going for … yes, a beautiful place we imagine being … but more importantly, a path to get there that we love exploring.

If the principles in this book are true, which I hold that they are, then what has kept us as a society from finding them? Perhaps it is the lies that we hold as self-evident … that we hold as the truth, even though history has proved them to be false.

THE 4 GREATEST LIES OF SUCCESS

The following are what can be called "cultural paradigms," meaning they're the hidden rules of society. Sometimes they're in our faces, placed there by our parents or other authority figures. Other times they're just the rules of the road … not so bold, but always there.

By referring to them as "lies," I'm not suggesting they're not valuable attributes or often required for the achievement of specific goals. What I am suggesting is that these "rules" do not necessarily lead to success as society would have us believe.

1. Desire Creates Success

Most people think that because they want something badly enough, they'll have the energy to get it.

Yet, how many people do you know who have a strong desire for a great deal more in their lives?

How many of them have had that desire for a long time?

And … how many are achieving it?

The fact is, almost everyone desires health, wealth, and happiness, and almost no one achieves all three. How many people do you know who even have two?

Desire only creates the yearning for something, but it has none of the actual magical energy it takes to stay on the path toward achieving it.

2. Hard Work Creates Success

How many people do you know who have been working hard their whole lives? If you worked twice as hard as you do now … if you worked twice as many hours every day …

would you be successful? (Or would you be divorced or dead?) Hard work is, of course, a good thing. It just doesn't guarantee success.

3. Being a Good Person Creates Success

Be a good person. I am not advocating anything else. But what does being a good person have to do with at least financial success? How many financially successful jerks do you know? Haven't you seen the evidence that "money has no conscience"? Money doesn't care where it goes. Neither does health, and in many domains of knowledge, neither does wisdom.

4. Getting a Good Education Will Lead to Your Success

The more actual education we can get in life, the better. Yet the world is filled with educated derelicts. Education does not guarantee that you will get what you want.

So what does lead to the good life? What will naturally propel you toward your goals and keep you in momentum and having fun?

If thousands of people have found the secret to success, it's got to be Self-Motivation.

Self-Motivation is the combination of physical, emotional, spiritual, and mental energies that move us to *act and attract*, such that we make progress on our chosen paths. We easily choose to do the things we know we must do. Every day, we "vibrate" at a frequency that allows us to attract what we need, and we open ourselves up to *see what we need to see* to find our way. This is Self-Motivation. This is the secret to success.

☑ This is Winning.   ☑ This is Happiness.

☑ This is Success.   ☑ This is Mach2 With

☑ This is Living.   Your Hair on Fire.

CHAPTER 3
THE POWER OF SELF-MOTIVATION

"SELF-MOTIVATION IS THAT MAGICAL CONCOCTION OF
EMOTIONAL, SPIRITUAL, PHYSICAL AND CREATIVE
ENERGIES THAT LAUNCH US INTO ACTION."

— Richard Bliss Brooke

Ask yourself this:

If you could get yourself motivated enough ...

And keep yourself motivated enough ...

What do you think you could achieve?

Another way to define Motivation, other than acting, attracting, and seeing, is in its more practical forms. There are many, but here are the five main ones.

The 5 forces of Self-Motivation

ENTHUSIASM
COURAGE
PERSISTENCE
PHYSICAL ENERGY
CREATIVITY

1. Enthusiasm

The word comes from the Greek word "entheos," which means "God within," and the "iasm" is often referred to as "I am sold myself."

This one simple energy can fuel you to accomplish most anything all by itself. Think about the daily "must dos" that a lack of enthusiasm can keep you from doing, and for which an abundance of enthusiasm makes it naturally easy. Think about the workouts, the meal choices, the prospecting, the studying, or the practice required to achieve the goal. What could you accomplish if those daily or weekly "must dos" were naturally effortless?

Think about how powerful you are when you are enthusiastic about these things. What could you accomplish if you got yourself and kept yourself enthusiastic enough about the process?

Can you list 3 things you have done daily with enthusiasm that led to success?

_____

_____

_____

2. Courage

Courage is not a genetic quality. Courage is a state of mind and heart. Courageous people see the same dangers as others do. They just act anyway. They "make up" something different about their ability to be successful.

Courage shows up hugely in the "must dos" of prospecting, whether you're in real estate, mortgage sales, fundraising, or Network Marketing. If you can prospect effortlessly, fluidly, naturally, and powerfully, then you know you will be as successful as you choose to be.

But what do we do when we think of a prospect and courage is in short supply?

We "chicken out" by making up something about the outcome that sends us packing. Our path to success is full of Ys in the road. One path leads to success, the other to frustration. At each Y in the road we get to be a chicken or a champion. Courage is essential for champions.

What are your stories when you recognize danger on your path to success? Ever notice that when you are compelled to "Do It Anyway," you make big stuff happen?

Can you list 3 things you were scared to do but were compelled to do anyway?

_____

_____

_____

3. Persistence

Every worthwhile venture will be riddled with setbacks. We will get knocked down … sometimes so hard that it takes everything we have to just see the possibility of getting up again. Motivated people not only see getting up again, they bounce off the mat. They _have_ to get up again.

So think about not only your life, but also the lives of others you know. Who do you know that could have enjoyed enormous success had they just been able to pull themselves up off the mat one more time? When have you quit short of success? Perhaps you will never know what you missed.

Notice how the man or woman who wins is the one who never stops … not necessarily trying the same thing over and over again, but rather, never stops creating, never stops problem solving, never stops relaunching, and never stops learning.

Can you list 3 times when you felt like quitting, but you got back up?

_____

_____

_____

4. Physical Energy

Everything we set out to do requires it. Some goals, like finishing the Ironman competition, require trainloads of it. The Ironman requires a 2.4-mile swim, 112-mile bike ride, followed by a 26.2-mile run. Hundreds of people who are first-timers do this in 60-degree water and 100-degree heat. I know people in their sixties who have done it for the first time.

Can you imagine competing in that race? Can you imagine how much more physical energy you would need than you have now? Can you imagine the training regimen of two to four hours each day for four to twelve months?

Iron men and women summon the physical energy to pull it off, and it is not genetic. It is pure Motivation. They do it because they create the *energy* to do it. We can all create energy and apply it to our daily tasks.

Can you list 3 physical things you easily feel like doing that others may find hard?

_____

_____

_____

5. Creativity

There are two distinct forms of creativity as it applies to Self-Motivation:

PROBLEM SOLVING

You and I solve problems by putting our brains to work on solutions. Our innate creativity looks for ways to solve problems, which is sometimes adding 2 plus 2 to equal 5. Sometimes it's just finding a new perspective or a new way of saying something that moves us forward.

One way of looking at achieving any goal is to say that the only thing standing between where you are now and where you want to be is a series of problems. Solve the problems and you progressively achieve more of the goal.

Creativity solves problems. Creativity is not genetic. Even the most brilliant people in history are, or were, only marginally smarter than any of us. The most brilliant are just vastly more motivated.

What are the problems that stand in your way?

Can you list 3 problems you have yet to solve?

_____

_____

_____

You can solve them. Motivation can solve them.

RED LIGHTS, YELLOW LIGHTS, GREEN LIGHTS

Red Lights, Yellow Lights, and Green Lights are simply creative interpretations. We have the creativity to "see" things in a certain light or with certain color glasses. When we see things in the light of:

I can do it
It will work out
They will enjoy what I have to offer
This will be fun
This will be easy

We get a Green Light and nothing will stop us from acting on it.

When we "make up" an outcome that does not look easy or fun or successful, we get a yellow light—caution—and this leads to procrastination. Procrastination is the kiss of failure.

And when we make up that an outcome is actually going to be bad, scary, or embarrassing, we see a Red Light and we hit the brakes, avoiding the risk altogether. _Roadkill._

An example worth millions in itself is in prospecting for new clients or associates. When a motivated person "sees" a prospect, they naturally "make up" that approaching the prospect is a good thing, and that it will work out for both parties. Seeing it that way leads them to make a comfortable, easy, fun, and most important, a confident approach … and make it right away. The result will always be better than a scared, timid, forced approach, or obviously no approach at all.

How many prospects have you "creatively" avoided over the years? How much momentum and progress do you think it may have cost you?

What if you could get yourself and keep yourself "turning on the Green Lights" on your path? What could you accomplish? How fast could you get it done?

Can you list one goal you have where you consistently see Green Lights?

_____

One with Yellow Lights?

_____

One with Red Lights?

_____

Creativity is not the exclusive property of genius. Creative thought is the direct result of being motivated.

The combination of all these energies "firing" at the same time creates a vibration that brings to us good fortune. It is quite literally our "power to produce." And … each of these 5 forces is available to us on demand, anytime we want, in extraordinary quantities. **It is our Vision that determines when and how we unleash this incredible power.**

CHAPTER 4
WHAT IS A VISION?

"THE THREE DEGREES OF VISION: POSSIBLE ... I WILL TRY.
PROBABLE ... I WILL STAY WITH IT. INEVITABLE ... I WILL WIN."

— Richard Bliss Brooke

A Vision is an expectation, mindset, belief, or an outcome. It is what you hold as *inevitable*. We have Visions (expectations, mindsets, and beliefs) for everything we can imagine ourselves doing, whether we have ever done it or not. They include how we act and feel in any given set of circumstances.

We base them on our experiences and our imagination. Our Visions are little movies we play in our minds. They may be very clear and visual, or vague like trying to tune into a bad TV channel.

We have millions of them. Everything you and I can ever *remember* doing, having, or being, we have a Vision for. And everything we can *imagine* ourselves doing, having, or being, we have a Vision for.

They make up who we are. They are what we use to move in the world … either toward something or away from something.

We think in words, which we convert to pictures, which we convert to memories or associations, which we then convert to feelings.

I have a Vision about me playing baseball. When I was in the fifth grade I got hit by a pitch … probably a 20-mph fifth grader's pitch. But it hurt, and it scared me. It embarrassed me. These are powerful feelings for a fifth grader. I have rarely played baseball since.

If you say the word "baseball" to me, I visualize the game, and I remember getting hit, and I feel the fear. It happens in a nanosecond. It leads me to avoid playing baseball, or if I do, I am always afraid of getting hit, so I play poorly. Does that make sense? That is my Vision of me playing baseball … even 55 years after being hit by one single pitch.

I would have a Vision of me playing baseball even if I had never played and never been hit … through association. I have seen it played. I know what it looks like. I can imagine myself playing it. That imagination is my Vision. What might influence that imagination is anything about baseball I have ever seen, anyone I know who has played it, books I have read, movies I have watched, and other sports I have played. Everything "out there" influences my "in here."

If my parents had loved baseball and watched games and had favorite players and played it themselves, their conversations and their feelings would have also influenced my imagination.

Think of how immensely powerful our minds, bodies, emotions, and spirits are to record all of these events and charge them with feelings. And to be able to imagine even more … far more … and attach feelings to them as well.

WE BUILD OUR VISIONS FROM THREE BASIC SOURCES:

Actual experience: This is what has happened to us. This is real. This really happened. We can prove it. It is our experience. This is really powerful stuff. The best movies are true stories.

What has happened to you that has shaped who you are and how you think? Take a moment and write them down. Seeing them on this page will help you see the impact that experiences have.

1. _____

2. _____

3. _____

4. _____

5. _____

6. _____

7. _____

8. _____

9. _____

10. _____

What authorities say: This is our parents, our teachers, people we respect, and the news (or at least it used to be). Anyone we view as knowing more than we do shapes our own beliefs and expectations. What they say matters to us.

Who were the authorities in your life? Who still are? What do they believe that you tend to believe? Write them down here.

Who: _____

Belief:_____

_____

Who: _____

Belief:_____

_____

Who: _____

Belief:_____

_____

Who: _____

Belief:_____

_____

Who: _____

Belief:_____

_____

What we say or our imagination: You may call it self-talk, affirmations, or imagination. It is what separates humans from the rest of the animal kingdom. We have the ability to make things up. We have imagination. We get to decide what to think about. We go beyond instinct to conscious thought. It is how we have built the world we have. Look around you. What have dogs built? Ants? Birds? Fish? Beyond nests and families … nothing. Humans can create anything they choose to think about … whether that ends up being a good thing or not.

And this, my friends, is the richest source of input. We talk to *ourselves* far more than anyone talks to us. Not 100 times more. Not 1,000 times more. Infinitely more. Constantly more. All of the time. Nonstop. *Blah blah blah blah, yadda yadda yadda* into oblivion. Right?

Listen to it. Pay attention to it. What does "it" say? How does it make you feel?

What are some of the things you say to yourself … about yourself?

Good Things

1. _____

2. _____

3. _____

4. _____

5. _____

6. _____

7. _____

8. _____

9. _____

10. _____

Bad Things

1. _____

2. _____

3. _____

4. _____

5. _____

6. _____

7. _____

8. _____

9. _____

10. _____

"IF YOU TALKED TO OTHERS THE WAY YOU TALK TO YOURSELF,
WOULD YOU HAVE ANY FRIENDS?"

— Rick Warren

"IMAGINATION IS THE ART OF CREATION. IT IS WHAT SEPARATES US FROM EVERY OTHER BEING. WE GET TO 'MAKE UP' OUR LIVES. WE GET TO CHOOSE."

— **Richard Bliss Brooke**

The breakthrough point here is to understand that you, me, all of us, **we make it all up**. We make up like a fairy tale what we decide is true. And we change our minds all the time. One day the sky is blue, and the next day it is red. One day the bear talks and gives us some of his honey, and the next day he roars and chases us. We invent everything. Sure, it is influenced by our past, our authority figures, and our "I AM-ing" declarations in our developmental years, but we still make it up.

And in the moment we are telling the story, we swear it is true.

Even swearing it is true is something we make up.

SO NOW WHAT?

The opportunity is to MAKE UP something that inspires you, builds belief in you, edifies you, loves you, fires you up, creates confidence, and gives you clarity. We are humans. We get to decide. We get to choose our thoughts. You can paint a mess or a masterpiece … your choice.

Notice what you are saying to yourself even after reading this. Do any of these fit?

I can't.

I don't know how.

I am just the way I am.

I have always been this way.

I have tried before, and it didn't work.

You made them up. Notice how they keep you stuck. Do you like being stuck?

Or maybe you made up something like this:

I can.

I will.

I will change.

This time I am ready.

I will have fun changing.

I will keep working with it until I have a breakthrough.

LITTLE CIRCLE, BIG CIRCLE

Little Circle/Big Circle is where experiences combine with self-talk to create a quantum leap in belief and Vision.

It works like this. Something happened, like me getting hit by the pitch. It happened one time in the fifth grade, decades ago. It lasted all of 30 seconds. I was not injured, just a little scared and embarrassed. One time. One event. Not that big of a deal. Little circle.

But then what did the infinitely creative human do with the little circle? He made it a big one. How? By making up stuff about it … all kinds of little mind-movies … all dramatic and such.

Here is what it sounded like:

The other boys are laughing at me.

I look weak.

I cried, and they think I am a baby.

I am scared.

I am scared it will happen again.

I am scared the ball will hit me when I try to catch it.

Nobody wants me on their team.

My friends don't like me.

The girls don't like me.

My parents are concerned.

Do I need to go on with the Big Circle? This is all stuff I made up. No one ever said or acted out these things. I *decided* they were true. I combined a real event with many imaginary ones. Big-Circle Vision.

These are the mindsets we have. These are our beliefs. These are our expectations. These stories are what lead us to act … or not.

As you can see, we have usually been somewhere between unconscious, casual, and reckless in how we have crafted our stories.

Think of these stories as code. They are, in a very real sense, how we have programmed ourselves to function. Garbage in, garbage out. All hardware is pretty much the same. The power of the computer is in the software … the programs.

Change the code, and you change the function.

We are embarking on changing the code.

CHAPTER 5
THE SECRET TO SUCCESS

"BECAUSE I CRY IN A MOVIE I KNOW IS NOT REAL, I CAN
ACCOMPLISH ANYTHING TO WHICH I SET MY HEART'S DESIRE."

— Richard Bliss Brooke

It is actually not a secret. In fact, it has been known and taught since the ancients. For some odd reason though, it has struggled to become mainstream. When I first learned of these concepts and laws, the first thought I had was: *How could algebra be more important than this? Why is it not taught to every 15-year-old? Why are there not master's degrees in this?*

I don't know. Maybe it scares people. Maybe the power of it leaves people in awe. It did me.

Before I tell you the secret, let me create some context. I will keep it simple. The science of the mind can get complicated, fast.

There are, what I am going to call, two "mind" parts to us. There is the conscious mind and the subconscious mind.

The conscious mind is the part that provides reason, judgment, and discernment. It learns the answers to tests, it learns hot and cold, and it learns whether running out into traffic is a good idea or not. It is what we use to go to school, get a job, succeed at work, mow the lawn, argue about politics, brush our teeth, etc. In monetary value, it might be worth upwards of $200,000 a year. But it's fairly useless in terms of accomplishing great things. It does not move mountains or propel us toward our dreams. If you are doing any of that, you are using much more than your conscious mind.

The second part of the mind is usually referred to as the subconscious mind. It is normally credited with all of the power. I am going to suggest that we are more than that … and that we have far more power available to us than just our subconscious mind.

I call it The Infinite Spirit, or the "IS." This is a literary-license term. You may call it God, or you may just add God into the mix. Either way, it is where the magic is. Here is what I suggest makes up the Infinite Spirit:

Subconscious Mind. This is our creative genius bar, our autopilot, and our nuclear reactor all in one. This is where we solve the problems, paint the masterpieces, build the skyscrapers, write the billion-dollar code, and conduct the philharmonic orchestra. This is the part of us that pumps the blood, breathes, repairs our diseases, and charts the course we set (Visions). This thing as a computer is worth trillions.

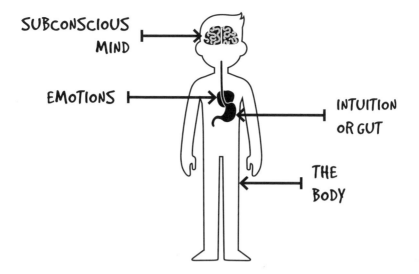

Emotions. The essence of us is feelings. Everything we do is either to pursue a good feeling or avoid a bad one. We are ***feeling beings***. Whether we are looking to power away from something or bring it into existence, our emotional tour de force is awe-inspiring. Hurt our feelings and we may make it our life purpose to destroy you. Make us feel good and we will cherish you forever.

Intuition or Gut. It is now known as a "mind" … just as (or more) powerful than the one in our heads. Crazy enough, but this mind is not made up of grey matter. It's made of microbes … somewhere between 40–400 trillion of them. How many is that? The entire earth has about 3 trillion trees. These microbes live in and on our bodies. They are very smart bugs. They know things. They know truth. They speak to us. We must listen.

The Body. It is a magnificent thing, again made up of cells, about 37 trillion of them. It's capable of miracles … in healing and heroics. Here is just one example.

In 2015, James Lawrence, father of five, completed … count them …

> *50 Ironman competitions in*
>
> *50 consecutive days in*
>
> *50 different states.*

That is a 2.4-mile swim followed by a 112-mile bike ride followed by a 26.2-mile run.

Followed by … get on a plane and fly to the next state. 50 days in a row. His nickname is "The Iron Cowboy." He shows us what is possible.

Now with this context, here is the secret:

THE SECRET TO SUCCESS

To the degree there is clarity, our Infinite Spirit (IS) does not distinguish between an actual experience and one that has been vividly imagined.

What that means is when the "IS" experiences something virtually—visually in our imaginations—it cannot tell the difference between that virtual reality and *actual* reality. To our "IS," it is as though it really happened.

Remember, our Infinite Spirit is not our conscious mind. Our conscious mind knows very well the difference, and it will be quick to tell us the difference.

Try this proof on yourself.

Name a movie that, for you, was very sad:_____

Remember the movie. Close your eyes even and visualize watching the movie. Can you feel yourself being moved just by the thought? Can you feel the sadness? If you watched the movie again, would you cry?

Name a movie that terrified you: _____

Visualize the worst scene if you can. Feel the earth move?

Name a movie that gave you immense joy: _____

Can you go there and feel it?

All of these movies featured vividly imagined moments that you—your body, your mind, and your soul—reacted to as though they were real.

Sure, your conscious mind knew all along that none of it was true … that none of it was real. Yet your SPIRIT was moved, your emotions emoted, and your body twisted and turned and coiled and hummed just as though you were living the movie. You grabbed your seatmate in terror, you cried with sadness, and your whole body, mind, and spirit sang with joy. Why was that? Because your Infinite Spirit could not tell the difference.

This scenario demonstrates how our conscious mind "knows" things, but those things don't really matter much. And when the powerful part of us is subjected to a movie that moves us … it moves us. We respond as though what's playing in our heads and hearts is actually real. Even if we don't want to respond, we do anyway … every time. It's true.

A vividly imagined experience has the same programming quality and impact as an actual, "real" experience.

To the Infinite Spirit, they are the exact same thing!

How does that create the Secret to Success?

Think about it. If the part of you that is most powerful—infinitely powerful—worth trillions of dollars and could compete in an Ironman every day … if it cannot tell the difference between you *actually* being someone you want to be, having things you want to have, and doing things you want to do versus just *imagining* it, then how about we start imagining it?

Imagine that what your Infinite Spirit had been "experiencing" about you was that you ate fresh and clean every day because you studied food and physiology and because you loved it. Imagine that was who you are—that was your niche, your claim to fame, and your passion.

How many times a day can you imagine that? This is a serious and breakthrough question. How many times? 10? 100?

If you just visualize it 10 times a day, to your Infinite Spirit it is as though you ate fresh 10 times today. What if you did it again tomorrow and every day for 30 days? That would be 300 "experiences" of a fresh, clean meal that you loved. That is 90 days' worth of eating clean and fresh.

Question: What do you think you would be motivated to eat on day 91?

What if you visualized for the Infinite Spirit that you were a master connector and networker? What if you wrote and watched a movie of you naturally, and with great confidence and authenticity, connecting with new people every day? What if who you were for those people was a servant leader, a therapeutic listener … the *most interesting person* they had ever met?

What if you "experienced" it 10 times a day for 30 days? That is 300 powerful conversations. What do you think you would tend to do with your NEXT conversation opportunity?

This virtual reality opportunity *is* the Secret to Success. We can MAKE UP any perfect process, state of being, skill, attitude, or destination, and our Infinite Spirit will pursue it like we have always been that way. It is a miracle. It is free. We all have it.

This creates both an opportunity for an extraordinary life or one of struggle. It is a very sharp two-edged sword.

"IT IS NOT IN THE STARS TO HOLD OUR DESTINY BUT IN OURSELVES."

— William Shakespeare

The power is in our chosen words. Our language. The pictures we choose. Our intentions. Every word we utter. Every word we imagine. Every picture we see triggers an emotion. It lights a fire in us to produce what we want or what we don't want.

NOTES

CHAPTER 6
THE GOLD IS IN THE GAP

"STRETCH THAT TENSION BETWEEN WHAT IS AND WHAT YOU DEMAND, AND WATCH YOURSELF LAUNCH INTO ACTION."

— Richard Bliss Brooke

The connection between Vision and Motivation is hardwired. It is a function of the way our brains and the rest of the Infinite Spirit systems work in the body.

The following statement communicates this as best I can:

To the degree that there is a gap between our Vision and our current reality (results), MOTIVATION naturally, effortlessly, powerfully, and infinitely flows to close the gap.

It does this instantly, as soon as it recognizes that a contrast exists. The best analogy for how this works is a thermostat.

Let's say the actual temperature (reality) is 65 degrees, and you set the thermostat to 70 degrees (your Vision). There is a contrast between them. So, the thermostat signals the heater to produce heat (motivation) until the temperature hits 70 degrees, at which time the thermostat signals the heater to stop. If it is cold outside (LIFE) the temperature in the room starts to cool back down almost immediately.

When it drops below 70 degrees, Motivation (heat) begins to flow, and the warming-up process begins again. Back and forth, back and forth, the temperature rises and falls, constantly in search of 70 degrees. (Thank you, Bob Proctor, the most prolific coach on this subject—www.BobProctor.com.)

So, when what *is* happening in your life contrasts with what you decide *should* be happening, the "thermostat" in your mind releases Motivation to bring the two together to create alignment. As the two come together, Motivation is momentarily reduced, only firing up again as they drift apart.

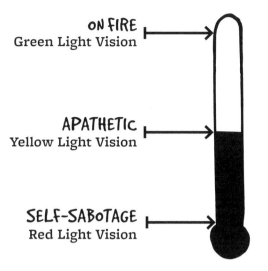

THE RELATIONSHIP BETWEEN YOUR VISION, SELF-MOTIVATION, AND WHAT YOU WANT (YOUR GOAL)

There are three basic forms of this relationship between Vision, Self-Motivation, and your Goal.

1. Self-Sabotage or Red Light Vision

This is where the temperature is 65. You want it to be 70, but you actually have your Vision set to **below reality** … like 60 degrees. Your belief or expectation is that your results are going to get worse than they are now, even though you want much more.

This is worry, negativity, and drama in action. This is subconsciously undermining your results. You want the temperature to come up to 70. It is currently 65 and you keep throwing water on the fire. You don't want to, but you cannot help yourself.

2. Apathetic or Yellow Light Vision

This is where your Vision is not aligned with what you want; it is more in line with what your current reality is. You may want it to be 70 degrees, but your Vision is more like 65 degrees. The actual temperature is also 65 degrees. It does not matter what you want the temperature to be. You have set the thermostat to where the temperature is already. This creates nothing more than apathy. It may also look like coasting or laziness. It may also create frustration—you want something but notice you are consistently not motivated to pursue it.

3. "On Fire" or Green Light Vision

This is where your Vision (the thermostat setting) is aligned with what you want—your goal. Let's say they are both at 70 degrees. No matter what the actual temperature is, Self-Motivation will pour forth to close the gap. If the actual temperature is 65 degrees, heat (motivation) will come on to bring it up to 70. If the temperature is 80 degrees, cooling (motivation) will come on to bring it down to 70. In this case, your Vision and goal are the same. This is ideal and results in you being "on fire" about doing what you need to do to close the gap.

Let's see how this all plays out in some common scenarios. For simplicity's sake, we'll be using a scale of 1–10 in these examples …

RELATIONSHIPS

We want a more harmonious, honoring, and loving relationship. We want it to be a 10. We want to say the right things and do the right things. We know what to do. We know the "love language" we need to speak. **This is our goal**.

Our relationship is a 7. **This is our reality.** We mess up too often, saying and doing petty and selfish things.

Our Vision is actually a 4. We imagine that our mate does not trust us, love us, or honor us. We blame them. We worry that we will mess up. We think in negative drama. We want them to do for us first, then we will do for them.

We are motivated to screw up. We say petty things, and we blame and argue for no good reason other than the fact that we are addicted to being right.

This is a Red Light or Sabotaging Vision.

DIETS

We want to get fit and lose fat and inflammation. On a scale of 1–10, we want to be at a 10. **This is our goal.**

Right now, we are at a 5. **This is our reality.**

We "see ourselves and expect ourselves" to be more like a 5 than a 10. **This is our Vision.** When it comes to the daily things we know we need to do to get fit, we more often than not see ourselves slipping, procrastinating, or rationalizing why we can get by "just this one time" with eating junk.

We have a Yellow Light Vision … apathy, procrastination, or rationalization.

Our Vision, more often than not, matches our *reality*. We are, at best, apathetic about our fitness. And remember, THIS HAS NOTHING TO DO WITH WHAT WE WANT. We are actually motivated to maintain the 5, even though we want the 10.

We find ourselves eating junk without even noticing we chose to eat it. There we are all of a sudden with an open bag of chips … now half a bag left. We find ourselves "getting busy," and all of a sudden, the day has gone by and we did not work out. We find ourselves saying yes to dining out, socializing, and of course, ordering accordingly.

This is why diets do not work. It does not matter what pill you buy or what gym membership you choose or what powder you mix up for breakfast. **If your Vision is a 5, you eat too often at Five Guys (my favorite burger joint).**

BUILDING A TEAM OF CUSTOMERS OR SALESPEOPLE

We want to build a big sales team, recruiting lots of customers and salespeople. We want to be at a 10. **This is our goal.**

Our **current reality** is that we have a small team and we are not recruiting many new customers or salespeople. We are at a 5.

Our Vision is also at a 10. It matches our goal: to build a big sales team. We see ourselves as a powerful leader. We see the abundance. We feel it. We know we deserve it. We know we need to talk to people in an authentic and powerful way each day. We know we need to be curious and listen. We take advantage of every opportunity to connect with people, we build service-based relationships, and then when the opening is clear, we ask them to buy or to join our team. We are ON FIRE about where we are going, and we are *in love with the daily process.*

We have a Green Light Vision.

And this is, of course, what we want. We want to harness the power of our Infinite Spirits to unleash:

> *Enthusiasm*
> *Courage*
> *Persistence*
> *Physical Energy*
> *Creativity*

We want to do the little things required in every moment … the tiny, easy-to-make decisions and not-easy-to-make decisions that lead to what we want.

Notice how in this matrix, what you and I want *is* a vital component … it gives us direction, but it does little or nothing to sustain the effort.

"THE ONLY THING WORSE THAN BEING BLIND IS HAVING SIGHT BUT NO VISION."

— Helen Keller

Here is how this system played out in my money-making efforts. When I started out in my new "big money" business opportunity, I started with a Vision that I could not make that kind of money. I *wanted* to make it. I *hoped* I could make it. I *wished* somehow I would get lucky. And I didn't want anyone to know that I didn't think I could do it, so I *tried*.

I worked really hard; I invested everything I could get my hands on. I traveled everywhere, learned everything I could, and I made $12,000 my first year. Then I made another $12,000 my second year. (This is the same income I earned as a chicken chopper.) Then I got tired of working so hard, so I took it a little easier and earned $4,000 my third year.

You see, even though I wanted to earn big money, and I did everything I could think of to do it, I was working against an anchor dropped years earlier: a life-limiting "I AM" of "I am not good enough." I thought I didn't need anybody, including the greatest minds of our time. This is a bad position to be in when you're supposed to be building a network of thousands.

In those early days, I expected to fail. That was my unconscious goal, and I "achieved" it again and again, much to my dismay. I "creatively avoided" talking to hundreds of prospects, easily making up that they would not be interested or that I would look bad by asking them to "just take a look."

When I *tried* to talk to someone, I'd say something like, "Gee, I don't know if you'd be interested, but maybe you'd like to hear about this part-time opportunity ..."

Deep down inside, I didn't really believe that anybody in his right mind would join me—and it showed. My recruits were few and far between. Most failed to excel and dropped out after a short time. Try as I might, I could never manage to enroll that top-level sales performer who would catapult his lucky sponsor (me) to overnight riches.

So finally, after losing everything I had, including my home, three cars (repossessed), all my credit, and worst of all, my pride, I finally hit bottom and woke up. With the fear of returning to the chicken plant a failure, I decided to implement what had been taught to me three years earlier.

I went to work on my thoughts and what I held to be true … literally changing my mind about what I had decided about myself. It wasn't easy, but it was just as simple as the decisions I'd made early on. I just decided to be different and to do different things, and then I kept deciding those new decisions over and over and over again until they caught hold. And then, all I did was hold on!

It worked. Within six months, I was earning $10,000 per month. Within two years, I was earning almost $40,000 per month.

So you might ask … *what did you actually do differently?* I did this: I developed what Walt Disney called the "Art of Imagineering." I created a new Vision … one my conscious mind knew was not true but that I *trusted* my Infinite Spirit could hear and feel. And it did.

I started every day with a chapter of Napoleon Hill or a bracing dose of some other motivational book or tape. I read *As a Man Thinketh* by James Allen; *Psycho-Cybernetics* by Dr. Maxwell Maltz; Og Mandino's *The Greatest Secret in the World*; *The Magic in Believing* by Claude M. Bristol; *The Science of Getting Rich* by Wallace D. Wattles, and more.

All day long, I would repeat positive affirmations to myself, programming my Vision to expect success. I recorded my Visions on "sleep tapes" and listened to them all night long. I put the most on-fire motivational speeches I could find on full volume every morning to fire me up. I listened to two tapes, *The Power of Goalsetting* by Paul J. Meyer and *The Strangest Secret* by Earl Nightingale, perhaps thousands of times each.

At times, I felt like an idiot. Was this really me? The perennial skeptic? The cynic? Was I really behaving like all those wacky "positive thinkers"?

Yes, I was. And in no time at all, my new regimen began to bear fruit—just a little fruit, but it was enough.

A LITTLE MOTIVATION GOES A LONG WAY

The subtleties of Motivation are profound. It does not take a lot of it to influence our thoughts, which in turn influence our actions.

We are all presented with opportunities nonstop in our lives. People, places, and things flow by us in an endless parade of possibilities. We see some and don't see others … in fact, most pass us by like Casper the Ghost … completely invisible.

Remember: one of the functions of the Infinite Spirit is to *open us up* to see what we normally would not see. It is called our reticular activating system. We start seeing the things that were already there but that we had previously deemed not important enough to see. We see opportunities and we see them in a way (Green Lights) that we act on them. We make up scenarios where we can win. And then we GO.

HERE'S MY GREEN LIGHT STORY:

In 1979, a man named Jerry Schaub called me to buy some more of my product. He lived in Cedar Rapids, Iowa. I was living in Des Moines about 3 hours away. He wanted a product that cost $15. I would profit $5. It was the middle of February. And there was an ice storm going on.

Before reinventing my Vision, I would have given Jerry Schaub a red light. I would have "made up" that driving through a 3-hour ice storm to see him would not be worth it, that it wouldn't work out. At best, I would earn $5 for 6–7 hours of work. At worst, he would no-show. *I would not have gone.*

But I made up something different that day … something with bright green lights. I found myself positive and very creative.

I *decided* that if I drove all the way to Cedar Rapids that he would appreciate it so much that he would buy a case … $180 versus $15.

I *decided* that if I got there before noon, he would invite me to lunch.

I *decided* that if I had an hour with him, he might ask about my opportunity.

Decisions are simply things we make up that we hold as true.

So I drove through the ice storm.

Notice the subtlety of it all. That one decision: *to drive or not to drive.* It didn't take very much Motivation for me to decide to drive.

"CHOICES ARE THE HINGES OF DESTINY."

— Edwin Markham

I arrived at about 11:45 a.m. at the Village Inn. He was there. He invited me to lunch. Halfway through lunch, he asked me if there was any money in this opportunity. I told him in such a way that he believed—big-time.

Jerry joined me. He was not me. Jerry was one of the few people in life who grew up empowered. He must have had amazing parents. Every opportunity he saw with me, he converted to Green Lights. He asked me what to do. I told him. He did it. He earned me about $100,000 in the next year. In the next 3 years, I found 3 more Jerrys. Why? Because he had made me a true believer in myself.

By the time I was 28, I was earning $40,000 a month with 30,000 salespeople on my team. That was 1983. Six short years from the chicken plant. Four short years from *go time.*

The drive was worth it.

Pick an area that is important to you … income, family, health, or wealth.

Where were you 4 years ago in that area?

Describe it: _____

_____

Rate it on a scale of 1-10 compared to where you would LOVE to be:

_____

If you do not do something radically different, where will you be 4 short years from now?:

_____

_____

CHAPTER 7

HOW DO I GET RID OF THAT NASTY VISION?

"ARGUING WITH YOUR CONSCIOUS MIND IS LIKE PLAYING CHESS WITH A PIGEON. THE PIGEON JUST STRUTS AROUND THE BOARD, POOPING AND KNOCKING OVER ALL OF THE PIECES WHILE DECLARING ITSELF THE WINNER. A WASTE OF TIME."

— Richard Bliss Brooke

Whether you know it or not …whether you want it to or not …your body works without you "thinking" about it.

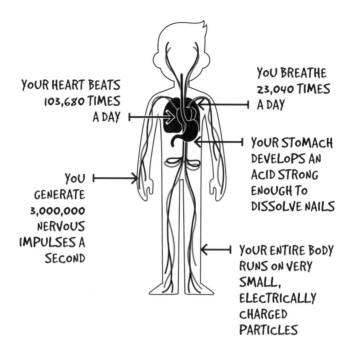

YOUR HEART BEATS 103,680 TIMES A DAY

YOU BREATHE 23,040 TIMES A DAY

YOUR STOMACH DEVELOPS AN ACID STRONG ENOUGH TO DISSOLVE NAILS

YOU GENERATE 3,000,000 NERVOUS IMPULSES A SECOND

YOUR ENTIRE BODY RUNS ON VERY SMALL, ELECTRICALLY CHARGED PARTICLES

YOU ALREADY HAVE VISIONS THAT MOTIVATE YOU TO DO WHAT YOU ARE ALREADY DOING.

Once you understand the relationship between Vision, Goals, and Self-Motivation, you may start to wonder: *How do I get a Vision, or how do I change one?*

This is a short but pivotal chapter. Getting the "how and why" to change your Vision is simple and yet critical.

The keys lie in a few simple ideas:

1. **There is a place within us that holds our Visions.** You might see it as your subconscious mind, your body, your gut, or the whole Infinite Spirit. It does not matter where you decide your Visions are kept, just as long as you understand they are in you. I prefer to see this place as a row of jars on a shelf. Each Vision is in its own jar, and there is a Vision for anything and everything.

2. **Essential to this understanding is that there is a Vision in each of the jars.** None of them are empty. If you can conceive it, then it has a jar. And as Napoleon Hill said, we can believe it (the Vision). And I repeat: none of the jars are empty.

"WHAT THE MIND OF MAN CAN CONCEIVE AND BELIEVE, IT CAN ACHIEVE."

— **Napoleon Hill**

3. **You have a Vision for everything you can imagine.** Therefore, it is never about getting a Vision. You already have one. If you want to know what it looks like and sounds like, just look at your most recent string of results. Look at what you have a tendency to do. That is your Vision. You might as well write it out, collect pictures and movie clips, find music to accompany it, post it up on your wall, and study it every day. If you think about it, that is a scary enough thought to motivate anyone to change it.

4. **We are all motivated, all of the time, by our Visions.** We are either motivated to move toward our goals, motivated to maintain the status quo, or motivated to sabotage things. Motivation is constant. It is like breathing, digestion, circulation, and healing. The Infinite Spirit is always alive and working, whether we are paying attention or not. We are always Motivated to **close the gap**.

5. **One of the neuroscience laws that we have to deal with is this:** THE SUBCONSCIOUS MIND CANNOT HOLD TWO OPPOSING THOUGHTS AT THE SAME TIME. What does that mean? It means that we cannot see ourselves failing and at the same time succeeding. We cannot see ourselves weak and powerful at the same time. We cannot see ourselves happy and sad at the same time. We can flip back and forth, but we cannot hold the opposing thoughts together. The jars cannot hold oil and vinegar at the same time. The jars can only hold one flavor of Vision at once. They do not mix well. It is black or white, or in this case, Green, Yellow, or Red … there are no rainbows in the jars.

6. **You cannot empty the jars.** You cannot dump out the old Vision and pour in a new one. You cannot tell the old Vision to "go away" or "shut up." You cannot

tell the old Vision, "You are wrong; I really am successful." You cannot run it off, invalidate it, shut it up, or vaporize it. There is only ONE way to replace an old Vision with a new one.

7. **You have an unlimited supply of Vision.** What separates humans from the purely instinctive animal kingdom is our ability to create thought. We have the gift of making things up. We can make up a story about anything we choose. I trust you get this by now. But add to it this … we can also tell ourselves that story as many times as we choose. Choosing what to think is a 24-hour-a-day opportunity with 1,440 minutes of opportunities to tell ourselves whatever we want. That is 86,400 seconds a day to fill with words we create. We can even influence this while we sleep by what we feed our minds before sleep and what we play in the background while we sleep. We can choose to dwell on our old Vision or we can choose to dwell on our new Vision.

Let's say you have two infinity pitchers that you can access at any time. One holds water and the other holds vinegar. In one of your jars on the shelf is vinegar. This is your old Vision, the one you don't want. How you establish a new Vision is by simply CHOOSING to pour the water into the jar far more than you choose or allow the pitcher of vinegar to go in. One displaces the other. There is no other way to do it. Grasp the infinite pitcher and pour it in. Pour it in until your new Vision fills the jar, displacing the old, and then KEEP pouring it in until it is a habit, until your results prove the theory of your Vision, until it is a part of your DNA.

Remember that your Infinite Spirit cannot tell the difference between a real experience (vinegar) and one vividly imagined (water). So to the part of you that moves mountains, holding that jar of crystal-clear water is real. Your conscious mind may know that you made it up and that you have always been nothing more than vinegar, but your conscious mind is no match for the Infinite Spirit … and the Infinite Spirit holds that jar as The Truth.

The transformational thing about Vision is it is infinite. You can create it in infinite abundance. The thing that happened once, you can relive 1,000 times. The thing you *imagine* once, you can have happen to you 1,000 times.

CHAPTER 8
IMAGINATION

"VIRTUALLY EVERYTHING WE SEE IN THIS WORLD THAT WAS NOT HERE 5,000 YEARS AGO WAS MADE FIRST IN THE MIND OF MAN. WE RULE THE WORLD FROM OUR GIFT OF IMAGINATION."

— Richard Bliss Brooke

Think about what you want. It is an easy question to ask, not always easy to answer. So let's tackle it. As G.K. Chesterton once said, "There are no rules of architecture for a castle in the clouds."

There are three basic forms of want:

1. **What do you want to have?**
2. **What do you want to do?**
3. **What do you want to be?**

And then the real driver behind all of them is: HOW DO YOU WANT TO FEEL?

Remember, *we are feeling beings*. We seek pleasure, or we seek to avoid pain.

Imagination is that gift of free thought. We have the gift of being able to choose what we think about—we can choose to imagine a fairy-tale life, a life we design.

So given that we have this gift, let's use it. Tell me a story. Make it up.

WHAT IF?

What if you could *have* anything you want?

What if you could *do* anything you want?

What if you could *be* anything you want?

Notice how you want to create the story, how you have an urging to make up a stunning masterpiece, but something keeps tugging on the purse strings.

We all possess this trillion-dollar computer capable of creating a blockbuster movie, but in most cases, we have a stranglehold on it, like we are hooking it up to a dial-up modem. We are driving a 200-mph supercar, and we keep it stuck in first gear. Our racehorse is hobbled.

Why is that? Remember the decisions you made as a 5-year-old? Remember all those "I AM" statements?

I am not enough

I am worthless

I can't

I am bad

I am not loved

I do not deserve

Remember those? That's your dial-up modem.

Notice how just as you want to express some creative ambition, you get stuck.

HERE ARE SOME EXAMPLES:

I want to be skinny and rich.

What comes next: *You have never been skinny, and you will never be rich.*

I want a loving, exciting, and safe love life.

What comes next: *You are not worthy of such fairy-tale lies.*

I want to lead a huge team.

What comes next: *No one will listen to you. Why would anyone follow you?*

I want a $2,000 pair of shoes.

What comes next: *No one should ever pay $2,000 for a pair of shoes, you fool.*

These self-defeating affirmations are what keep us from expressing the full power of our imaginations.

BUT … you can do an easy workaround right here.

What if you could *have* anything? And what if no one, including you, had any negative judgments about what you wanted?

What if you could *do* anything? I know you probably can't, but what if you could?

What if you could *be* anyone and anything? I know, people would laugh, and you may look once again the fool, but what if you could, and everyone actually championed you?

There is power in the **What If.**

Practice it now.

Make a list. Put everything on it that you want to HAVE, even if they're just things. No judgments.

1. _____

2. _____

3. _____

4. _____

5. _____

6. _____

7. _____

8. _____

9. _____

10. _____

What do you want to DO?

1. _____

2. _____

3. _____

4. _____

5. _____

6. _____

7. _____

8. _____

9. _____

10. _____

What do you want to BE?

1. _____

2. _____

3. _____

4. _____

5. _____

6. _____

7. _____

8. _____

9. _____

10. _____

Outside of this book, if you want to exercise your racehorse, rev your supercar, and spool up your supercomputer, make a list of 100 in each category. Just keep adding to each list until you get to 100.

Imagination is like a muscle. Use it or lose it. We have been given this gift. Everything you see in the man-made world, every invention, painting, sculpture, song, movie, science, and philosophy began in one man or woman's mind. They imagined it first. Edison imagined light. Michelangelo imagined painting the Sistine Chapel. Karl Benz imagined the modern automobile. Steve Jobs imagined Apple. Jeff Bezos imagined Amazon. Walt Disney imagined Mickey.

If you are ready for big changes in your life, start going to the imagination gym. Make the list. 100 each. You will be pleasantly amazed at the power it gives you.

"IF YOU CAN DREAM IT, YOU CAN DO IT. ALWAYS REMEMBER THAT THIS WHOLE THING WAS STARTED BY A MOUSE."

— **Walt Disney**

CHAPTER 9
WHO ARE YOU?

"WE ARE ONE OUT OF 7.7 BILLION. NO ONE LOOKS JUST LIKE US. NO ONE TALKS JUST LIKE US. NO ONE CERTAINLY THINKS AND FEELS JUST LIKE US. OUR AUTHENTICITY IS AN UNDERSTATEMENT. IT IS THE RAREST OF GIFTS. OWN IT."

— Richard Bliss Brooke

Our project in this book is to support you in understanding the relationship between all of these internal forces and then equip you with the tools for harnessing them.

The number one tool you will use is a new, conscious, intentional Vision that you design on *purpose*. This is the movie starring YOU … a NEW YOU.

You will use this Vision to drive out the old. You will use it to change your body chemistry. You will use it to spool up the Motivation—the Enthusiasm, Courage, Persistence, Physical Energy, and Creativity—to do those daily little things that compound into a new you and a new life.

Before you start writing the movie of your life, you will want to take a good look inside. You will want to ask the question: *Who am I? Who am I, really?*

Most of us live inauthentic lives …. not intentionally; it is just kind of the nature of our species. We are born into a strange world. We are looking for meaning. We are looking for love. We are looking for acceptance. And we are a clean slate. We do not prefer or believe in anything. We are not religious. We are not political. We do not fear anything except loud noises and falling.

The people we are looking to for these things are already in the world and already have beliefs and preferences. And they tend to want everyone else to agree with them. Why not? Being right is an addiction and getting people to agree with us validates us. Remember, our parents were once 5 too.

So here we are, highly impressionable beings, looking for love and acceptance. The giants in our world that hand out such things have strong opinions about life. They prefer that we should agree with them.

You can be who you **should be**. Or you can be who you **choose to be**. Choosing consciously is being authentic.

In my *Mach2* Video Series and "Live Your Bliss" workshops, I guide people through the process of distinguishing between their Authentic Values and those they may be holding as "shoulds" … someone said they *should* value it.

As we wind this Vision and Self-Motivation project up, you will be focusing on writing a New Vision. You want it to be as powerful as possible. You want the Motivation you unleash to push the least weight or pull the lightest load. You don't want to work to have something, do something, or be something that is not authentically you. You don't want to set goals you think you *should* set instead of goals you authentically want for yourself.

EXAMPLES:

- Avoiding pursuing financial gain because you were taught that you *should* be "humble and modest," and that people with wealth are evil, bad, or selfish.

- Pursuing wealth because you were taught that you *should* be wealthy or else you are not important.

- Avoiding fun, adventure, and play because you were taught that you *should* be responsible, and that fun is frivolous.

- Pursuing being skinny because you were taught that you *should* be skinny to be attractive.

- Avoiding finding a strong, successful spouse because you were taught that you *should* take care of yourself.

- Pursuing finding a rich spouse because you were taught that you *should* find someone to take care of you.

- Avoiding higher education because you were taught that you *should* stay home and take care of the kids.

- Pursuing higher education because you were taught that you *should* get as much education as you can no matter what.

The point of these examples is that none of them are right or wrong. They are preprogrammed responses to the authority figures in our lives telling us what *their* values are and that ours should be the same.

Sometimes we authentically agree with those choices and sometimes we do not. When we do not authentically want something for ourselves, but we attempt to do it anyway, the "should" is like an anchor we drag with us. We are trying to do something we really do not want to do.

"BE YOURSELF. EVERYONE ELSE IS TAKEN."

— Oscar Wilde

It's like we're the wizard in *The Wizard of Oz*. We spend so much time and energy frantically fumbling around behind the curtain, trying to convince people we're something we're not, that we never let our authentic selves shine. For the wizard, it took curious little Toto to pull back the curtain, and for you, it will take identifying what's truly important to you … and ONLY you.

To prepare you in writing your new Vision, the following exercises will bring to the front of your mind what is important to you.

VALUES

What are your values?

Take some time right now to review this list and sit with the question for a bit. What are the most important things to you in life? This is a sample list. You may label your values with any words that speak to your soul.

- Acceptance
- Appreciation
- Belonging
- Comfort
- Intimacy
- Respect
- Safety
- Security
- Fun
- Peace
- Spirituality/God
- Honesty
- Humor
- Independence
- Integrity
- Relationships
- Creativity
- Family
- Freedom
- Trust
- Work
- Communication
- Excellence
- Pleasure
- Power
- Recognition
- Joy
- Love
- Order
- Partnership
- Harmony
- Participation
- Contribution
- Health

Write down your 5 most important values from the list or use your own. If you end up with more than 5, that is fine, but the more you can narrow them down, the more focus and sense of priority you will have. Just because a value does not make the top 5 does not mean you do not hold it as dear. You still value it. Just get as concise as you can.

1. _____

2. _____

3. _____

4. _____

5. _____

Congratulations for getting this done. You are starting to form a clear profile of the Authentic You.

GIFTS

Each of us has one or more natural gifts or talents that are contributions to other people. You may be in denial about yours, but just ask someone who knows you well. I believe these gifts were awarded to us for a reason—so that we can share them with the world. And, I believe that we are most powerful when we are sharing the special gifts that we are.

For the same reason we want to craft a new Vision with our authentic values, we also want to craft one featuring our gifts. Think of it as though we are the star of our movie and the storyline is that we are the hero. Think about what superpower this hero has. What will the hero use to save the day, to create this new life? What is his or her gift?

Here are some examples of gifts. Again, whatever you want to call your gift is perfect. These are just examples.

- Storytelling
- Contribution
- Creativity
- Ability to Make Friends
- Fun
- Honesty
- Inspiration
- Integrity
- Imagination
- Empathy
- Leadership
- Listening
- Love
- Music
- Writing
- Sense of Humor
- Athleticism
- Organization
- Spirituality
- Enthusiasm

Write down 3 of your gifts in order of their strength.

1. _____

2. _____

3. _____

Congratulations. You are making awesome progress!

STRENGTHS

Leverage your strengths. Leverage your *BEING*.

Most of us have been taught to pursue success by identifying what we want to do. We want new cars and we want to travel the world. Our tendency is to go directly for those things and the money that will provide them. And yet, our greatest point of leverage to achieve anything and everything we want is not what we have, but WHO WE ARE. It is who we are, and who we are being in the moment, that creates the tangible results in our lives.

People who are broke, sick, or friendless are so because of who they are *being*. What they have done to create those results is simply an effect that follows the cause.

Your *Mach2* movie has to star you. The most powerful Visions are those that redefine who you are—where you envision yourself as a person who deserves happiness, health, and wealth … a person who attracts it like the powerful magnet you are.

You have strengths. You have qualities. You have character. It will serve you to get in touch with them, own them if you will, bring them to the party. Like your values and gifts, your strengths are important attributes of your movie. Let's make them part of the storyline.

Imagine we are sitting around with a small group of people who love and champion you. They know you for your strengths. Imagine I am asking them to tell me what they love about you, what they admire about you, what it is about you that inspires them to be better? Imagine I am listing all of these things on a giant whiteboard.

Imagine we are asking you the question, "Why WILL you be successful?"

Now you do it.

Make a list of your top 10 strengths. They may include talents, beliefs, attitudes, skills, connections, credibility, and/or specialized knowledge.

1. _____

2. _____

3. _____

4. _____

5. _____

6. _____

7. _____

8. _____

9. _____

10. _____

THEME OF YOUR LIFE

This last piece is kind of like the theme song of our lives, our personal purpose for being here. Life purpose is often confused with doing something grandiose, like finding a cure for cancer. Grandiose accomplishments may be an authentic life purpose for some, but for most of us, the theme of our lives is much simpler. For example: raising a successful family, being a role model for the community, inspiring others to succeed—these might be authentic, powerful life purposes for many.

Discovering and wordsmithing your life purpose is an ever-evolving project. Start now. Give it a go. Think about how you want to be remembered. Think about where your groove is. Think about your *bliss*. If you were to follow it, where would you go?

Take a few minutes to ponder it, then write something down.

The theme of my life is:_____

_____

_____

_____

_____

No matter what you wrote here, congratulations. It is a start, which places you ahead of 99.9% of everyone else.

"YOU CAN IGNORE YOUR BLISS. YOU CAN FOLLOW YOUR BLISS. OR YOU CAN BE YOUR BLISS."

— **Richard Bliss Brooke**

CHAPTER 10
LASER, LEVERAGE, AND LOVE

"YOU CAN LIGHT A ROOM, BOIL WATER OR CUT THROUGH STEEL. WHAT DOES YOUR VISION REQUIRE?"

— Richard Bliss Brooke

Congratulations. If you have done these exercises, you know more about who you are than probably 10,000 other people. Most people never go through this kind of self-analysis looking for what is important to them—and *only* them—looking at their gifts and strengths, and then looking at what they want to do with the rest of their lives.

You are now in a powerful position to organize all of this into CHOOSING CHANGE.

Success comes through us before it comes to us.

Refer back to your lists from Chapter 8 of things you want to have, do, and be. And remember, your maximum leverage to getting and doing things is to focus on who you can *become*. The more you become, the more you get to do, and the more choices you have in *what* you can have.

Now let's narrow the focus. You probably know that unfocused light may illuminate a room, but when you focus light, it can cut through steel.

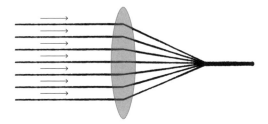

Let's focus your light.

If you could **have** just *one thing* … one material thing in your near future, one thing that would make a huge difference to you, what would it be? And what if you could have it no matter what you or anyone else said? What would it be?

_____

If you could **do** just *one thing*, one accomplishment, one adventure, one contribution, what would it be? One thing that would bring you the most joy, peace, and power. What if you could do it no matter what you or anyone else thought? What would you do?

_____

If you could **BE** different, if you could become someone new … with some new qualities, beliefs, attitudes, skills, and habits, who would you become? Who would you become that would bring you the most **feeling**. Who would *move you*? Who could you become that would automatically carry the day on the first two goals … material thing and accomplishment? In other words, if you just focus on the Becoming, the Being, the New You, who could you become that would, by virtue of that becoming, have the things you want and do the things you want?

Here is an example:

> *What if what I really want to HAVE is a new, fancy car?*
> *What if what I really want to DO is travel the world first class?*

Then by focusing on the highest leverage point and turning light into a laser …

Who could I BECOME that would automatically be driving a new car and traveling the world?

Instead of focusing on the new home or the new car or first class, let's focus on transforming the *being* that will earn those things.

This creates massive leverage.

What if you focused all of your light on:

Your listening	Your responsibility
Your leadership	Your patience
Your love	Your generosity
Your attitudes	Your learning
Your beliefs	Your humility
Your work ethic	Your productivity
Your respect	Your consistency
Your maturity	Your creativity

Are you starting to see the picture? Is a Vision forming? Are you starting to see and feel a new you?

Are you ready to pour some secret sauce on it?

FALLING IN LOVE WITH THE PROCESS:
THE SECRET SAUCE

One of the most powerful secrets to manifesting your new Vision is to pay less attention to the actual outcome (the beautiful end story) and pay far more attention to the process.

For example, if your Vision is to walk across your country, say 3,000–5,000 miles, you could, of course, visualize the celebration and the accomplishment of having done it … and I encourage you to do so in living color.

But the most powerful part of that end Vision would be the Vision of the process. The process is you walking 10–50 miles a day, every day, regardless of the weather, terrain, equipment failures, or any mental games you may be inclined to fall victim to.

Imagine that you paint a beautiful story of who you are … and what you do is WALK EVERY DAY. If you walk every day, when that is *who you are* and *what you do*, you WILL get to the end … one mile at a time.

Everything has a process. When you focus on a Vision of yourself successfully executing the process, it leads to the process being the habit … and we are all in love with our habits.

This is the holy grail of manifesting: falling in love with the process. What are the "processes" that would lead you to manifesting your Vision?

If it is health you are after, what are the daily processes, the choices, the habits you need to nail every day? Imagine falling in LOVE with doing them. You can. You and I can fall in love with anything when we intend to, and we do it every day. We ARE in love with our habits. We are addicted to them. And we can learn to feel this way about the daily zone we need to be in.

If it is an extraordinary relationship you want to manifest, what are the things you need to do every day to make it happen?

If it is a sales achievement, what are the daily to-dos? How many people do you need to approach every day? How do you need to approach them, and who do you need to BE every day to manifest your dreams?

Here are some simple examples:

Longevity: Eat fresh and eat less every day

Fitness: 10,000 steps every day

Loving Relationship: Speak their love language every day

Spirituality/God: Meditate or pray every day

Sales/Business: Listen to one new prospect every day

Can you see how focusing on who we are and what we do every day systematically leads to what we want … the end-game? *Live longer. Be more fit. Empower our love life. Connect to our God. Build our business.*

COMPOUND YOUR GOAL TO MAKE LASTING CHANGE

Einstein called compounding "the eighth wonder of the world." This is how the rich get richer and the poor get poorer. (It is also how you can make lasting, significant change in your life.)

Consistency and time are the keys to compounding.

If you double a penny every day (consistency) for 30 days (time), it compounds to be worth over $5 million dollars.

DAY 15	DAY 21	DAY 26	DAY 30
$163	$10,500	$335,000	$5 Million

 AFTER 30 DAYS, ONE PENNY BECOMES OVER $5 MILLION!

If you double it every other day, in 30 days, it is worth $163.84

Day 1	$0.01	Day 17	$2.56
Day 3	$0.02	Day 19	$5.12
Day 5	$0.04	Day 21	$10.24
Day 7	$0.08	Day 23	$20.48
Day 9	$0.16	Day 25	$40.96
Day 11	$0.32	Day 27	$81.92
Day 13	$0.64	Day 29	$163.84
Day 15	$1.28		

Likewise, many of our goals can be achieved through compounding.
Eating habits, workouts, how we speak to and treat other people, and how we approach any kind of habit-building relies on consistency—and consistency compounds.

Here are a few examples:

Eating. Think about our diet goals. If we eat right only every other day, our bodies get confused. Our taste buds only get trained to go back and forth from fresh to processed over and over again. We never gain any traction or momentum. Consistency is not present, and our eating habits do not compound.

Yet if we eat fresh and clean every day, we train our bodies to respond, to demand fresh and clean, to be motivated by fresh and clean. The weight comes off, and that motivates us even more. We gain traction and momentum. A consistent diet compounds.

Fitness. Think about our workouts. If they are consistent, they build on each other. Each one gets to use the strength of the previous one. Our workouts get more intense yet easier. Our bodies start to once again demand to be worked. The habit gets instilled, and we gain traction and momentum. Workouts compound.

Love Language. If our partners can rely on our words and deeds consistently speaking love, then love grows. If we are on-and-off—encouraging then discouraging, loving then apathetic—we fail to build trust. We undermine the love. Consistency of our words and deeds gets traction and momentum. Love compounds.

Map this onto **focusing on ONE THING** that you can do every day that will for sure lead you to becoming who you want to become … having it all and doing it all.

If you harness all of your Motivation and focus it on the One Thing, and if you fall in love with that one thing, then you dramatically increase the probability that you will do it every day. And if you do it every day, you are building a 5-million-dollar habit. If you do it much less than every day, you are building a $163 habit … which do you want?

CHAPTER 11
CHOOSING THE NEW YOU

"CAN YOU CHANGE? HAVE YOU EVER CHANGED?"

— Richard Bliss Brooke

It is time to choose. What will you do? What will you take on? What will be your new Vision?

Remember how many jars we have on the shelf? Millions. Hundreds of millions. It will serve you to take just one down and focus on displacing the Vision currently in it.

Pick a jar that will make the biggest difference in your life AND that you are ready to transform.

You have to be ready to change.

You have to be sick and tired of being sick and tired.

You have to be fed up … with fat or whatever else is in that jar.

You may have to be where I was … broke and driving a borrowed car.

Better yet, you have to be smart enough to make a move now before you pay any more of a price.

PICK NOW

Health/Fitness	Anger/Drama
Love Life/Relationships	Business/Income
Spending/Debt	Listening/Relating
Gambling	Fun/Adventure
Drinking	Giving/Service
Drugs	

Note: *If you are not ready to answer these questions, you are not ready to change. That is OK. It is your life; you choose to live it how it honors you. It is not for me to say or judge. If you are not ready, there is no point in continuing the book. Put it down. Pick it back up when you are ready to decide. It's OK.*

Or maybe these questions will make a difference. I call them the dark-side questions. Take however much time you need to answer them.

1. **What is staying the same costing you?**

    _____

2. **What is it costing you in income?**

    _____

3. **What is it costing you in love?**

    _____

4. **What is it costing you in peace?**

    _____

5. **What is it costing you in integrity?**

    _____

6. **What is it costing you in friendships?**

    _____

7. **What is it costing you in fun?**

    _____

8. **What is it costing you in expressing yourself?**

    _____

9. **What is it costing you in health?**

    _____

10. **What is it costing you in lifespan?**

    _____

Now are you ready to pick a jar? Which one will bring you the most joy and relieve the most pain?

Write it down here:_____

_____

NEXT, ANSWER THESE QUESTIONS:

What do you need to do every day, in every way, to unleash consistency and compounding on the process?

_____

What daily process will you fall in love with?

_____

Which of your authentic values will you be honoring?

_____

Which of your strengths will you be deploying?

_____

How will you use your gift as the tip of the spear?

_____

How does this harmonize with the theme song of your life?

_____

Remember to focus on the One Thing ... the One Thing you can do every day that can transform you, transform the people around you, and transform your life.

If you have answered these questions, you are ready to go.

CHAPTER 12

WRITING THE FILM SCRIPT OF YOUR LIFE

"WORDS CREATE THE PICTURES, WHICH TRIGGER THE MEMORIES AND ASSOCIATIONS ATTACHED TO FEELINGS. WORDS ARE THE ART OF MOTIVATION."

— Richard Bliss Brooke

The crafting of a new Vision is best done by following the model of a film script. Film scripts are written with the specific intent to create emotions in the viewers: fear, sadness, joy, and anger. A great movie leads the audience to "emote" how the writer and director intended for them to emote. That is your job here: to intentionally lead yourself to experience the emotions that motivate you … to feel how you will feel when you are actually immersed in the manifestation of your Vision.

Movies work for this because they cover the full gamut of clarity and detail. You have a detailed description in a film script of exactly what is happening and where it is happening: the season, the weather, the décor, and the people involved. There is a soundtrack … both music to lead you to emote and dialogue presented by great "actors." There are the sounds of nature, or the city, or whatever else the creative writer and director can think of that will lead you to feel the way they intend for you to feel.

Your NEW film script will not have any sadness, fear, anger, envy, sickness, or resignation. You have enough of those emotions.

New Visions are simply new film scripts. So if you want to get more fit, you would write a film script about you getting fit and the single daily ONE THING you are in love with to get that done.

You will want to ask (and keep asking) yourself: *What is the underlying feeling that I'm seeking?* Then express that feeling the most in your new Vision or "film script." How does being fit lead you to FEEL?

"Good and fine" won't cut it here. You need to go deeper. You need to allow yourself to imagine how you will feel when you are fit. See what words you can put on those feelings. The more precise the words, and the more ways you can describe the feelings of fit, the more power you will unleash to get on the path.

AFFIRMATIONS

Affirmations are the building blocks of Vision. They are the bullet points of "I AM-ing."

Below is a list of positive affirmations. Read through each one of them, preferably out loud. Circle your favorites. Add some of your own. Read them several times a day. Memorize them. Add them to a vision or dream board. Use them to inspire your Vision.

EXAMPLE AFFIRMATIONS:

I absolutely love myself.

I deserve happiness.

I am in action every day.

I give people my full attention.

I listen to people at a level that heals.

I am healthy and vital.

I have freedom.

I am massively productive.

I attract good fortune.

I am easy to be with.

People follow me with ease and confidence.

I deserve abundance.

I deserve health.

I am having fun.

I love supporting people.

I love vigorous exercise.

I am wealthy.

I have lots of free time.

I get things done anyway.

I attract whatever I need.

People love listening to me.

People love being with me.

I ooze confidence.

I believe in myself.

I know success is inevitable for me.

Life is fun for me.

I am safe and secure.

I believe in my goals.

Life is easy for me.

Life is abundant for me.

---

10 RULES FOR WRITING YOUR FILM SCRIPT

1. Find the sweet spot.

There is a sweet spot of Self-Motivation … a place where you can find the most traction to change and produce new results. It is "beyond boring" and just "short of miraculous." Call it sensational. When you manifest this Vision, it will be sensational! Pick the jar off the shelf that represents that sweet spot.

Visions that are borderline boring are those that we know we can accomplish without much of a stretch. They are perfectly believable. Yes, they are things we want that we don't have now, but when we see ourselves achieving them, they're a little too *meh*. Don't write about boring Visions. They will bore your soul … and you need to stir it.

Visions that are almost beyond believable and miraculous also pay diminishing returns. Anything in the unbelievable realm will be fought hard against by your current Visions.

You do not need to create miracles here. You can create giant baby steps. You can move with velocity by learning to believe in what you can see now, and then as you go and grow, you will see further and deeper into your future.

2. Clarity is power.

The shorter the experience, the easier it is to write what is happening. When you write about **who you are** and **what you are doing every day in every way**, it is easy to grasp. Make that the bulk of your Vision, and the end result just icing on the cake.

Remember: to the degree there is clarity, your Infinite Spirit—your subconscious mind, your emotions, your body, and your gut—cannot tell the difference between an actual experience and one vividly imagined. *To the degree there is CLARITY.* Clarity is in the details.

3. Always write in the first person.

This script is about you, seen through *your eyes*. Write it as such, using "I," "me," or "we" language.

4. Always write in the present tense.

This is a hugely important distinction and in contrast to goal setting. Goals are generally written as being accomplished in the future. Visions are always expressed as being accomplished right now. Not yesterday. Not tomorrow. Right now. The power required to kick your Infinite Spirit into massive action will not work with a goal or a history lesson. It will only respond to what you say must be so … right now. *I am this way now. I am. I am. I am. I am.*

5. Write in positive word pictures.

The mind responds to pictures, not words. It converts words to pictures and then pursues the pictures. If you want to quit smoking, you cannot say, "I don't smoke anymore." Your mind only sees a picture of you smoking and leads you back to it. You must describe who you are and what life is like as though there is no such thing as smoking … no word for it, no concept for it, no picture for it.

You are not losing weight. You are not paying off debts. You are not breaking any bad habits. You are only expressing the new you as though those things never existed.

6. Describe who the NEW YOU is.

Refer back to your answers from the last chapter and paint a beautiful picture of who you ARE. When you ARE deserving, valuable, worthwhile, and loving, you will manifest in accordance with that. Leverage your life by becoming the person who deserves it all.

7. Describe the environment.

Where is this success taking place? Movies do not happen in a vacuum. Set the stage. Describe the room if you are inside, the lay of the land if outside. What is the weather like? Is it day or night? Hot or cold? Describe it in enough detail that your mind can fill in the blanks and paint a vivid picture of how you want the environment to look and feel.

8. Describe the soundtrack.

Will music inspire this Vision? If so, what song are you listening to? Memorize the tune so you can "dance" to it while you visualize your movie. Is nature playing one of its tunes? If so, direct it to be so.

9. Create the dialogue.

What exactly are you saying and to whom? What are they saying to you? What are they saying to others about you? Write the script as you would love to have it play out. Add to every line the "tone" you intend for the "actors" to use. Is it excitement, gratitude, love, recognition, celebration?

10. Direct the emotions.

How do you FEEL in this new movie? How are you acting out these emotions? How do others feel about you and what you have accomplished? How do they feel about what they have accomplished?

The emotional part of the script is the most important because it is emotion that imprints our subconscious. It is emotion that motivates us. We want to feel a certain way, and we will move mountains to feel that way. Dig deep to find the right words to describe it.

As you embark on the journey of writing, be patient and gentle with yourself. As you attempt to write, or even think about what to write, you are starting a process of change to your core … change you may never have attempted before. You have 20, 30, 40, or maybe 80 years invested in who you are. You will not take kindly to changing overnight.

EXAMPLES OF VISIONS

WEIGHT LOSS/FITNESS

I stand tall and straight, exuding confidence.

Walking down the street, I feel powerful, strong.

When I catch my reflection in a window, I smile.

I twirl and love how I look from every angle.

My arms and shoulders are toned; my waist is trim.

Each step I take highlights my calf muscles.

My new dress feels great against my skin.

The sun catches my hair just right.

I am beautiful.

Birds are singing, a light breeze lifts me along.

I am free.

Movement brings me strength and energy.

I sleep soundly at night and wake up refreshed.

My body craves the fuel of fresh, whole food.

I love preparing healthy meals for my family and trying new things.

Slicing and dicing puts me in a zen place.

I can feel my cells forming a protective shield, keeping me young and healthy.

People say I look amazing.

They want to know my secret. I laugh and my eyes twinkle.

I deserve this health.

Life is good, as I choose it to be.

SALES/RANK ACHIEVEMENT

Crossing this stage,

I am smiling from the inside out.

The applause from the crowd fills the room.

I deserve this success.

I am a natural leader. I shine in this spotlight.

This is my moment.

People want to hear what I have to say.

I speak from my heart, confident, self-assured.

I am genuine; a person everyone wants to be friends with.

It's easy for me to approach people. I just DO IT.

Making connections is my purpose.

I am curious about other people and love to listen.

I hear, "You've changed my life" and it fuels my passion to serve even more.

I am in momentum; unstoppable.

BEAUTIFUL RELATIONSHIP

This is the person who fits me perfectly.

Every day, our bond grows stronger.

We are best friends, soul mates, loving parents.

I feel safe and totally at ease when we're together.

Our beautiful home is our sanctuary, a place of calm and happiness.

Talking with this person is my favorite part of the day.

I listen with my full attention; it is only us in the moment.

I make time for hugs and small touches.

Compliments flow freely between us, filling up our buckets.

I feel fully accepted and accepting of this person.

We love to laugh; it comes easily.

We have ever-increasing abundance in our lives – financial peace and prosperity.

We love to talk about our dreams.

We are moving in the right direction, together.

FINANCIAL ABUNDANCE

This check feels light in my hand.

Paper thin, yet oh-so powerful.

It is the first of many.

My heart soars with a sense of freedom.

Cash flows effortlessly toward me each month in a steady stream.

It fills me up with a feeling of peace.

I attract this just by sharing my gifts.

I serve people creatively and with great generosity.

I look for their needs and wants, and I empower them with new ideas.

I give freely, and it comes back ten-fold.

I enjoy extraordinary things that my willingness to change has brought me.

I am full of life and love and can manifest anything I choose.

BLISS LIFE VISION POEMS

If poetry stirs your soul and you want to move beyond one-liner affirmations, here are some "bliss life" vision poems you can memorize to bring clarity to your goal and inspire your daily journey. You can even use these as part of your own powerful Vision.

BEST LIFE VISION

I am one of a kind
With unique gifts to share
Adventures to have
Big dreams to dare.

I am fabulous, fun
Fearless and free
I have one life to live,
So I choose to be me.

I soar to each goal
Like a bird in flight
Warm sun on my face,
Weightless and light.

I'm worthy, wonderful,
My work feels like play.
I attract what I want
I'm ON FIRE each day.

I see it; believe it.
This new story of mine
I live a bliss life,
A life *I* design.

LISTENING VISION

I am attraction in action
People are drawn to me
I have a gift for listening,
Effortlessly.

My inner voice is quiet
I'm curious to the core
Just like falling in love,
I want to know more.

I stay in the present
Never skipping ahead
I am a Tai Chi Master,
Hearing the words unsaid.

I feel what they are feeling,
I hear what they have to say
Their story is the *only* story
It's all about them today.

I listen in a way that heals,
Reveals their open book
They want to get to know me,
They want to take a look.

I see it; believe it.
This new story of mine
I live a bliss life,
A life *I* design.

FITNESS VISION

I love what I see
When I look in the mirror
Each day as I move
My Vision gets clearer.

I am healthy and strong
I look great in my clothes
Every rep, every step,
My motivation flows.

My sweat powers me on.
Keep going, keep going!
I'm an exercise beast
The fire ever growing.

I see the finish line
I cross for the win
I'm steady; I'm ready;
I can do it again.

People notice my glow
I give off good vibes
I have mountains of energy,
I feel so alive.

I see it; believe it.
This new story of mine
I live a bliss life,
A life *I* design.

FAMILY VISION

I have a grateful heart

And love beyond measure

Endless gifts to give

To my family, my treasure.

Our home is a place

Where it's easy to laugh

We love to dream big

We're on the same path.

We have great abundance

Cash flow and fun toys

We love to share with others

To experience simple joys.

Each day I let them know

"I am on your team."

I listen with intention,

I build their self-esteem.

I take care of my body

Feel my energy grow

It's easy to play full out

My light is green, *let's go!*

I see it; believe it.

This new story of mine

I live a bliss life,

A life *I* design.

CHAPTER 13
ACTION ON THE SET!

"A VISION WITHOUT ACTION IS JUST A FANTASY."

— Richard Bliss Brooke

It's said that "a picture is worth a thousand words." My extension of that quote is ... a picture is worth a thousand words of CLARITY.

THERE ARE 3 LEVELS OF CLARITY:

Level 1: A written Vision

Level 2: A Vision board with a set of pictures and graphics

Level 3: An actual movie

HOW TO CREATE A VISION BOARD

A vision board is simply a visualization tool made of words, phrases, and pictures. You can build one physically that you hang on your wall, or you can create it online and make it your screen saver, for example. Or you can set a program to email it to you every morning and night.

Search the Internet and magazines, or even your own happy photos, to find images that best represent your Vision ... what your ideal life looks like, how you want to FEEL, and who you want to BE. You don't have to get too literal; just find images that speak to your soul. You'll know them when you see them!

Create an eye-pleasing collage of your images. Be sure to include your favorite affirmations, words, quotes, or snippets from a poem ... whatever moves you.

MAKING AN ACTUAL MOVIE

Make your Vision movie using iMovie or a similar platform. Look for pictures, quotes, video clips, music, and audio clips, anything that helps tell your story, and then integrate it with the written words of your Vision. If you do not know how to create something like this, ask for help. Most 12-year-olds are experts.

YOU will be the star narrator of this movie. Record your Vision in your own enthusiastic, inspirational voice, and combine it with your favorite song. This will be the soundtrack of your movie.

Keep working with it until when you watch it, it clearly moves you.

NOW WHAT?

So after you create all this wonderful stuff, what do you do with it?

At least twice every day, first thing in the morning and last thing at night, tune into your movie and look at your vision board. Say your favorite affirmations throughout the day whenever you get a chance.

Allow yourself to feel how you will feel when you are enjoying the new you. See and feel yourself stepping into it. Allow yourself to "pretend" that you are engaging in the processes, in love with the daily habits, being the new you, and celebrating your successes.

To your Infinite Spirit, this is like it is actually happening over and over and over again. It will learn to see it as *the truth*. It will respond accordingly that your truth must be manifested.

Every time you tap into the crystal-clear pitcher of water and pour it in, the vinegar disappears. Remember, they cannot occupy the same jar at the same time.

If you see yourself as healthy, you will naturally *be* healthy habits. If you see yourself as wealthy, you will naturally *be* wealthy habits. Let it unfold.

Actor and comedian Jim Carrey wrote himself a check for $10 million when he was at one of his lowest points. He signed it "for acting services rendered."

JIM CARREY $10,000,000

FOR ACTING SERVICES RENDERED

This method has NEVER failed anyone who has done it consistently. The imprinting process may work quickly for you or slowly for you, but if you stick with it, it will work for sure. The only way the imprinting process will not work is if you quit. If you quit pouring in the water, the vinegar will return.

As your new Vision TAKES HOLD, your mindset will elevate, creating that subtle yet powerful Motivation, which will positively impact all your actions and behaviors. Your performance in nearly every area of your life and work will change for the better. You will notice that you possess more and more courage, enthusiasm, confidence, persistence, passion, desire, and commitment … all of which are guaranteed to move your reality steadily and inevitably toward your possibilities. You will break through your barriers to success. You will experience the movie *Mach2 With Your Hair On Fire!*

Perhaps this all sounds pretty silly to you. Perhaps you're thinking it might be a fun project, but does it really work? Can it really work for someone like you? Believe me. It's not silly—it absolutely does work, and it will work for you.

HERE'S HOW IT WORKED FOR ME

In 1983, at a fair in Ohio, I purchased a mock-up of the cover of *SUCCESS* magazine with my picture on the cover. I framed it and hung it on my wall and looked at it every day. My Vision at that time was to be not only rich but famous as well. I wanted something to prove to my friends and family that I was really cutting it. *SUCCESS* magazine seemed like the perfect proof.

In March 1992 (almost 10 years later), *SUCCESS* magazine featured the Network Marketing industry's skyrocketing success as its lead story. It was the first time a mainstream publication had done so in the industry's 50-year history. Out of 50 million Network Marketers, they chose me for the cover and lead story.

Now, you may think this happened because I was the most outspoken, flamboyant, successful, or famous person in the industry. Not at all. Or, perhaps you think it was because I hired some public relations firm to make it happen. I didn't.

Actually, and rightfully so, *SUCCESS* wanted Rich DeVos, owner of the largest company in our industry, on the cover. Rich DeVos was about 1,000 times more successful than Richard Brooke. *SUCCESS* magazine thought he should be on the cover. He, however, did not return their phone call. You may think he did not return their call because he was too busy or because he didn't care. I don't think so. Rich DeVos did not return that call for only one reason ... I had the picture of myself on that cover. He, obviously, did not.

I want nothing more in the world than for people who take the time to read this book to actually do the work.

Miracles have come from it. And it is not my book that produces these miracles. It is the laws of nature and the science of the mind. Far more qualified experts have written about it long before I did.

I want to thank you with all my soul for reading my version. My Vision is that you will act on it and create your own miracle.

If you want to learn more about this work, I invite you to visit RichardBrooke.com.

BONUS APPENDIX
INSPIRATION

"INSPIRATION IS TO THE AMBITIOUS SOUL WHAT OXYGEN IS TO LIFE. WE CAN'T LIVE WITHOUT IT."

— Richard Bliss Brooke

I am a great believer in the power of inspiration to influence our own powerful Visions. The following are some of my favorites. Reading and reflecting on their wisdom allows me to feel the way I feel when I'm starring in the movie of my life. I encourage you to find and reflect on everything and anything that does the same for you.

THE FOUR AGREEMENTS

1. BE IMPECCABLE WITH YOUR WORD

Speak with integrity. Say only what you mean. Avoid using the word to speak against yourself or to gossip about others. Use the power of your word in the direction of truth and love.

2. DON'T TAKE ANYTHING PERSONALLY

Nothing others do is because of you. What others say and do is a projection of their own reality, their own dream. When you are immune to the opinions and actions of others, you won't be the victim of needless suffering.

3. DON'T MAKE ASSUMPTIONS

Find the courage to ask questions and to express what you really want. Communicate with others as clearly as you can to avoid misunderstandings, sadness and drama. With just this one agreement, you can completely transform your life.

4. ALWAYS DO YOUR BEST

Your best is going to change from moment to moment; it will be different when you are healthy, as opposed to sick. Under any circumstance, simply do your best, and you will avoid self-judgment, self-abuse and regret.

— Don Miguel Ruiz

The Four Agreements, (Amber-Allen Publishing, © 1997) Used with permission.

THE INVITATION

It doesn't interest me what you do for a living. I want to know what you ache for, and if you dare to dream of meeting your heart's longing.

It doesn't interest me how old you are. I want to know if you will risk looking like a fool for love, for your dream, for the adventure of being alive.

It doesn't interest me what planets are squaring your moon … I want to know if you have touched the center of your own sorrow, if you have been opened by life's betrayals, or have become shriveled and closed from fear of further pain.

I want to know if you can sit with pain, mine or your own, without moving to hide it, or fade it or fix it.

I want to know if you can be with joy, mine or your own, if you can dance with wildness and let the ecstasy fill you to the tips of your fingers and toes without cautioning us to be careful, to be realistic, to remember the limitations of being human.

It doesn't interest me if the story you're telling me is true. I want to know if you can disappoint another to be true to yourself. If you can bear the accusation of betrayal, and not betray your own soul. If you can be faithless and therefore trustworthy.

I want to know if you can see Beauty even when it's not pretty every day. And if you can source your own life from its presence.

I want to know if you can live with failure, yours and mine, and still stand at the edge of a lake and shout to the silver of the full moon, "Yes."

It doesn't interest me to know where you live or how much money you have. I want to know if you can get up after the night of grief and despair; weary and bruised to the bone, and do what needs to be done to feed the children.

It doesn't interest me who you know, or how you came to be here. I want to know if you will stand in the center of the fire with me and not shrink back.

It doesn't interest me where, or what or with whom, you have studied. I want to know what sustains you from the inside, when all else falls away.

I want to know if you can be alone with yourself, and if you truly like the company you keep in the empty moments.

— Oriah Mountain Dreamer

The Invitation, (Harper San Francisco, 1999)

THE DASH

I read of a man who stood to speak at the funeral of a friend.

He referred to the dates on her tombstone; her life from beginning to end (1934- 1998).

He noted that first came her date of birth and spoke the ending date with tears, but he said what mattered most of all was the dash between those years.

For that dash represents all the time that she spent alive on earth … And now, only those who loved her know what that little line is worth.

For it matters not how much we own; the cars … the house … the cash, what matters is how we live and love and how we spend our dash.

So think about this long and hard … are there things you'd like to change? For you never know how much time is left, that can still be rearranged.

If we could just slow down enough to consider what's true and real, and always try to understand the way other people feel.

And be less quick to anger, and show appreciation more, and love the people in our lives like we've never loved before.

If we treat each other with respect, and more often wear a smile … Remembering that this special dash might only last a little while.

So, when your eulogy's being read, your life's actions to rehash … Would you be proud of what they'll say about how you spent your dash?

— Linda Ellis

The Dash, (lindaellis.net, © 1998) Used with permission.

ALL I EVER REALLY NEEDED TO KNOW I LEARNED IN KINDERGARTEN

Most of what I really need to know about how to live, and what to do, and how to be, I learned in Kindergarten. Wisdom was not at the top of the graduate school mountain, but there in the sandbox at nursery school.

These are the things I learned …

Share everything.

Play fair.

Don't hit people.

Put things back where you found them.

Clean up your own mess.

Don't take things that aren't yours.

Say sorry when you hurt somebody.

Wash your hands before you eat.

Flush.

Warm cookies and cold milk are good for you.

Live a balanced life.

Learn some and think some and draw and paint and sing and dance and play and work every day some.

Take a nap every afternoon.

When you go out into the world, watch for traffic, hold hands, and stick together.

Be aware of wonder. Remember the little seed in the plastic cup? The roots go down and the plant goes up and nobody really knows how or why, but we are all like that.

Goldfish and hamsters and white mice and even the little seed in the plastic cup – they all die. So do we.

And then remember the book about Dick and Jane and the first word you learned, the biggest word of all: LOOK.

Everything you need to know is in there somewhere. The Golden Rule and love and basic sanitation. Ecology and politics and sane living.

Think of what a better world it would be if we all – the whole world had cookies and milk about 3 o'clock every afternoon and then lay down with our blankets for a nap. Or if we had a basic policy in our nation and other nations to always put things back where we found them and cleaned up our own messes. And it is still true, no matter how old you are, when you go out into the world, it is best to hold hands and stick together.

— Robert Fulghum

Bestselling Author, robertfulghum.com, 1988

THE OPTIMIST CREED

Promise yourself …
To be so strong that nothing can disturb your peace of mind.
To talk health, happiness and prosperity to every person you meet.
To make all your friends feel that there is something to them.
To look at the sunny side of everything and make your optimism come true.
To think only the best, to work for the best and expect only the best.
To be just as enthusiastic about the success of others as you are about your own.
To forget the mistakes of the past and press on to the greater achievements of the future.
To wear a cheerful countenance at all times and to give every living creature you meet a smile.
To give so much time to the improvement of yourself that you have no time to criticize others.
To be too large for worry, too noble for anger, too strong for fear and too happy to permit the presence of trouble.

— Christian D. Larson

Your Forces and How to Use Them, (LN Fowler & Co, Ltd.; London, 1912)

THE WAY OF TRANSFORMATION

The man who, being really on the Way, falls upon hard times in the world will not, as a consequence, turn to that friend who offers him refuge and comfort and encourages his old self to survive. Rather, he will seek out someone who will faithfully and inexorably help him to risk himself, so that he may endure the suffering and pass courageously through it, thus making of it a "raft that leads to the far shore."

Only to the extent that man exposes himself over and over again to annihilation, can that which is indestructible arise within him. In this lies the dignity of daring. Thus, the aim of practice is not to develop an attitude which allows a man to acquire a state of harmony and peace wherein nothing can ever trouble him. On the contrary, practice should teach him to let himself be assaulted, perturbed, moved, insulted, broken and battered – that is to say, it should enable him to dare to let go his futile hankering after harmony, surcease from pain, and a comfortable life in order that he may discover, in doing battle with the forces that oppose him, that which awaits him beyond the world of opposites.

The first necessity is that we should have the courage to face life, and to encounter all that is most perilous in the world. When this is possible, meditation itself becomes the means by which we accept and welcome the demons which arise from the unconscious – a process very different from the practice of concentration on some object as a protection against such forces. Only if we venture repeatedly through zones of annihilation, can our contact with Divine Being, which is beyond annihilation, become firm and stable. The more a man learns whole- heartedly to confront the world that threatens him with isolation, the more are the depths of the Ground of Being revealed and the possibilities of new life and Becoming opened.

— Karlfried Graf von Dürckheim, 1896-1988
The Way of Transformation: Daily Life as a Spiritual Exercise, (Allen & Unwin; London, 1988)

— QUOTES —

"Imagination is everything. It is the preview of life's coming attractions."
— Albert Einstein

"The real voyage of discovery consists not in seeing new landscapes but in having new eyes." — Marcel Proust

"Leap, and the net will appear." — John Burroughs

"Even if you are on the right track, you'll get run over if you just sit there." — Will Rogers

"There is only one place you need to go: your own heart. And only one thing you need to do: wake up." — Yogi Amrit Desai

"Sow an act and you reap a habit, sow a habit and you reap a character. Sow a character and you reap a destiny." — Charles Reade

"You miss 100 percent of the shots you never take." — Wayne Gretzky

"We hope vaguely but dread precisely." — Paul Valéry

"Life isn't about finding yourself. Life is about creating yourself." — George Bernard Shaw

"If you can hold it in your head, you can hold it in your hand." — Bob Proctor

"The intuitive mind is a sacred gift and the rational mind is a faithful servant. We have created a society that honors the servant and has forgotten the gift." — Albert Einstein

"This, therefore, is a faded dream of the time when I went down into the dust and noise of the eastern marketplace, with my brain and muscles, with sweat and constant thinking, made others see my Visions coming true. Those who dream by night in the dusty recesses of their minds wake in the day to find that all was vanity, but the dreamers of the day are dangerous men, for they may act their dream with open eyes, and make it possible." — T.E. Lawrence, 1888-1935, Introduction to Seven Pillars of Wisdom, (Oxford Edition, 1922)

"The Masters in the art of living make little distinction between their work and their play, their labor and their leisure, their minds and their bodies, their information and their recreation, their love and their religion.

They simply pursue their VISION OF EXCELLENCE at whatever they do, leaving others to decide whether they are working or playing. To them, they are always doing both!"— James A. Mitchner, 1907-1997, Pulitzer Prize Winning Novelist

"If I feel depressed, I will sing.

If I feel sad, I will laugh.

If I feel ill, I will double my labor.

If I feel fear, I will plunge ahead.

If I feel poverty, I will think of wealth to come.

If I feel incompetent, I will remember past success.

If I feel insignificant, I will remember my goals.

Today I will be the master of my emotions." — Og Mandino, 1923-1996, The Greatest Salesman in the World, (Bantam; Reissued Edition, 1983)

"Carefully watch your thoughts, for they become your words. Manage and watch your words, for they will become your actions. Consider and judge your actions, for they have become your habits. Acknowledge and watch your habits, for they shall become your values. Understand and embrace your values, for they become your destiny." — Mahatma Gandhi, 1869-1948

"Forces that threaten to negate life must be challenged by courage, which is the power of life to affirm itself in spite of life's ambiguities. This requires the exercise of a creative will that enables us to hew out a stone of hope from a mountain of despair." — Martin Luther King, Jr., 1929-1968, Strength to Love, (Harper & Row, 1963)

"If we don't change our direction, we are likely to end up where we are headed." — Chinese Proverb

"Amidst the glut of insignificance that engulfs us all, the temptation is understandable to stop thinking. The trouble is that unthinking persons cannot choose, but must let others choose for them. To fail to make one's own choices is to betray the freedom which is our society's greatest gift to all of us." — Stephen Muller, President Emeritus, Johns Hopkins University

"Every creative act involves … a new innocence of perception, liberated from the cataract of accepted belief." — Arthur Koestler, The Sleepwalkers, (Hutchinson, 1959)

"There are many who are living far below their possibilities because they are continually handing over their individualities to others. Do you want to be a power in the world? Then be yourself. Be true to the highest within your soul and then, allow yourself to be governed by no customs or conventionalities or arbitrary man-made rules that are not founded on principle." — Ralph Waldo Trine, 1866-1958, In Tune With the Infinite, (Kessinger Publishing, 1910 Edition)

"A midlife crisis is when you've reached the top rung of your ladder only to realize that you've leaned it against the wrong wall." — Author Unknown

"Far better it is to dare mighty things, win glorious triumphs, even though checkered by failure, than to rank with those poor spirits who neither enjoy much nor suffer much, because they live in the gray twilight that knows no victory or defeat." — Theodore Roosevelt, 1858-1919, From the speech The Strenuous Life, (Chicago, April 10, 1899)

"… I think it is a mistake to ever look for hope outside of one's self. One day the house smells of fresh bread, the next of smoke and blood. One day you faint because the gardener cuts his finger off, within a week you're climbing over corpses of children bombed in a subway. What hope can there be if that is so? I tried to die near the end of the war. The same dream returned each night until I dared not to sleep and grew quite ill. I dreamed I had a child, and even in the dream I saw it was my life, and it was an idiot and ran away. But it always crept onto my lap again, clutched at my clothes. Until I thought, if I could kiss it, whatever in it was my own, perhaps I could sleep. And I bent to its broken face and it was horrible … but I kissed it. I think one must finally take one's life in one's arms …" — Arthur Miller, 1915-2005, From the play After the Fall, (1964)

"When one door closes another door opens; but we so often look so long and so regretfully upon the closed door, that we do not see the ones which open for us."
— Alexander Graham Bell, 1847-1922, American Scientist & Inventor

"A pessimist sees the difficulty in every opportunity. An optimist sees the opportunity in every difficulty." — Winston S. Churchill, 1874-1965, British Prime Minister

"Surrender does not mean being passive; it means engaging yourself totally in what you are doing and then letting go of the outcome." — Yogi Amrit Desai, Doctor of Yoga and Holistic Healing.

"Security is mostly superstition. It does not exist in nature. Nor do the children of men as a whole experience it. Avoiding danger is no safer in the long run than outright exposure. Life is either a daring adventure or nothing at all." — Helen Keller, 1880-1968, The Open Door, (Doubleday and Company, 1957)

THE LAW OF RESPONSIBILITY

"Once we establish the limits and boundaries of our responsibility, we can take full charge of that which is our duty and let go of that which is not; in doing so, we find more enjoyment supporting others, as we create more harmonious cooperative relationships by understanding that which falls within the realm of our responsibility." — Dan Millman, Excerpt from The Life You Were Born to Live, (HJ Kramer, 1993)

"People, like nails, lose their effectiveness when they lose direction and begin to bend." — Walter Savage Landor, 1775-1864, English Poet

"If at the end … I have lost every other friend on earth, I shall at least have one friend left, and that friend shall be down inside of me." — Abraham Lincoln, 1809-1865, 16th President of the United States

"We cannot put off living until we are ready. The most salient characteristic of life is its coerciveness: it is always urgent, 'here and now' without any possible postponement. Life is fired at us point-blank." — José Ortega y Gasset, 1883-1955, Spanish Philosopher

"I have found the best way to give advice to your children is to find out what they want and then advise them to do it." — Harry S. Truman, 1884-1972, 33rd President of the United States

"With dedication to the rights of humanity with the empowerment of listening integrated with this Chinese philosophy that: 'There's nothing noble in being superior to someone else. The true nobility is in being superior to your previous self.'" — Reverend Peikang Dai

"It is not because things are difficult that we do not dare, it is because we do not dare that things are difficult." — Seneca, 5BC-65AD, Roman Philosopher

"You can be right or you can be happy." — Gerald G Jampolsky, M.D., Founder, Center for Attitudinal Healing, (Sausalito, California)

"For peace of mind, we need to resign as general manager of the universe." — Larry Eisenberg

"To-morrow, and to-morrow, and to-morrow,
Creeps in this petty pace from day to day,
To the last syllable of recorded time;
And all our yesterdays have lighted fools
The way to dusty death. Out, out, brief candle!
Life is but a walking shadow; a poor player,
That struts and frets his hour upon the stage,
And then is heard no more: it is a tale
told by an idiot, full of sound and fury,
Signifying nothing."

— William Shakespeare, 1564-1616, From the play Macbeth

"Success seems to be largely a matter of hanging on after others have let go."

— William Feather, 1889-1981, American Author

DARING GREATLY

"It is not the critic who counts; not the man who points out how the strong man stumbles, or where the doer of deeds could have done better. The credit belongs to the man who is actually in the arena; whose face is marred by dust and sweat and blood; who strives valiantly; who errs and comes short again and again; who knows the great enthusiasms, the great devotions, and spends himself in a worthy cause; who at the best knows in the end the triumph of high achievement; and who at the worst, if he fails, at least fails while daring greatly; so that his place shall never be with those cold and timid souls who neither know victory or defeat."

— Theodore Roosevelt, 1858-1919, From the speech Citizenship in a Republic, (Sorbonne, Paris; April 23, 1910)

"If I don't manage to fly, someone else will. The spirit wants only that there be flying. As for who happens to do it, in that he has only a passing interest."

— Rainier Maria Rilke, 1875-1926, German Poet

"It is in the nature of revolution, the overturning of an existing order, that at its inception a very small number of people are involved. The process in fact, begins with one person and an idea, an idea that persuades a second, then a third and a fourth, and gathers force until the idea is successfully contradicted, absorbed into conventional wisdom, or actually turns the world upside down. A revolution requires not only ammunition, but also weapons and men willing to use them and willing to be slain in the battle. In an intellectual revolution, there must be ideas and advocates willing to challenge an entire profession, the establishment itself, willing to spend their reputations and careers in spreading the idea through deeds as well as words." — Jude Wanniski, 1936-2005, The Way the World Works, (Touchstone Books, 1978)

THE MASTER GAME

"Seek above all, for a game worth playing. Such is the advice of the oracle to modern man. Having found the game, play it with intensity – play as if your life and sanity depended on it (they do depend upon it). Follow the example of the French existentialists and flourish a banner bearing the word 'engagement.' Though nothing means anything and all roads are marked 'No Exit,' yet move as if your movements had some purpose. If life does not seem to offer a game worth playing, then invent one. For it must be clear, even to the most clouded intelligence, that any game is better than no game." — Robert S. de Ropp, 1913-1987, The Master Game, (Delacorte Press, 1968)

"The tragedy of life is not death, but what dies inside us while we live …" — Norman Cousins, 1915-1990, American Editor and Writer

"People stumble over the truth from time to time, but most pick themselves up and hurry off as though nothing happened." — Winston S. Churchill, 1874-1965, British Prime Minister

"No problem can stand the assault of sustained thinking." — Voltaire (François-Marie Arouet), 1694-1778, French Philosopher & Writer

"You can't outwit fate by standing on the sidelines placing little side bets about the outcome of life… if you don't play you can't win." — Judith McNaught

"It is what you choose not to see in your life that controls your life." — Lynn V. Andrews

"Vision without execution is hallucination." — Thomas Edison

"Make your vision so clear that your fears become irrelevant." — Anonymous

"The universe never asked you to struggle. It is simply answering your mood." — Anonymous

"When I read the ghastly lines of tragedy darkly penned into my life, I turn and notice that the pen in my hand is wet." — Craig D. Lounsbrough

ABOUT THE AUTHOR

Richard Bliss Brooke is an ontological coach, transformational retreat leader, and keynote speaker. He is the author of *The Four Year Career®* and *Mach2: The Art of Vision & Self-Motivation*, and co-author of *The New Entrepreneurs: Business Visionaries for the 21st Century.*

Richard loves golf, Harleys, poker, boating, scuba diving, ATVs, and most recently, surfing. He also loves flying and is a passionate licensed aviator of both fixed-wing planes and helicopters.

Mostly he loves his wife, Kimmy. Together they run three multimillion-dollar global businesses from their own personal paradise in Lanai, Hawaii, including Bliss Business, a transformational coaching, workshop, and retreat organization.

You can read more about Richard and access his free trainings, blogs, self-awareness analyses, cartoons, and more at RichardBrooke.com.

CONNECT WITH RICHARD ON SOCIAL MEDIA & THE WEB

There's so much to LIKE when you become a fan of Richard:

- Be the first to know about upcoming events and the latest industry news
- Enter to win free products (including Richard's bestselling books!)
- Get inspired with Richard's videos, thought-provoking posts, and so much more

f facebook.com/RichardBlissBrooke

𝕏 twitter.com/RichardBrooke

▶ youtube.com/rbbrooke

in linkedin.com/in/richardblissbrooke

𝓟 pinterest.com/richardbbrooke

blissbusiness.com

Do you give up due to fear of failure or reliving past rejections? Do you lack clarity and direction when it comes to your goals?

THEN YOU WILL WANT ...

MACH2 VISION TRAINING

MACH2MOTIVATION.COM

This 4-step course breaks down the key steps to clarifying your vision and ultimately reaching the goals you've set for your life.

STEP 1:   READY, SET, LAUNCH ...

STEP 2:   THE POWER OF ...

STEP 3:   COURSE CORRECTION ...

STEP 4:   MANIFEST DESTINY ...

Take the next step to mastering your own mind and learning the art of self-motivation.

"MIND-BLOWN!

I just started the videos today because I wanted to finish the book once through before I started. I can't wait to make these changes. Wish I would have found this years ago!"

— Tracy Hughes
Westfield, Indiana

Ready to live a bliss life? During this 10-day audio series, you'll discover simple yet profound steps you can do immediately to elevate your mind, body, and soul.

SIGN UP FOR FREE

THE BLISS LIFE GUIDED AUDIO VISUALIZATION SERIES

BLISSLIFEAUDIO.COM

From acts of kindness to acts of forgiveness, success coach Richard Bliss Brooke will help educate you on what a bliss life is all about ... and how, by following these simple steps, you can alter your life forever.

▶ **LET GO OF WORRY**

▶ **HAVE MORE FUN**

▶ **IMPROVE RELATIONSHIPS**

▶ **ESTABLISH BOUNDARIES**

"I loved how these 10 Days were short with lots of info. Easy to fit into your day. They made you stop and think. I'm loving it ... Thank you!"

— Lee Briggs
Barnstead, New Hampshire

Take this 10-day journey and get on your way to bliss!

JOURNALING

JOURNALING

JOURNALING

JOURNALING